THE RHINO
STAYED FOR BREAKFAST

This is a true story about the day-to-day experiences of a young couple who set up home in Africa. Their first baby is due to be born within a few months, but owing to an acute housing shortage in Nairobi their attempts to find a place to live are at first unsuccessful.

Life in Kenya can never be very austere and even when Mau Mau, with all its horrors, comes down upon a small and unprepared community, life still continues to have its lighter side.

Day by day the shadows increase, and those who have made their home upon the high veldt in this country, where civilisation is no more than skin deep, find their lives darkened and inescapably changed.

Books by Rowena Lee in the
Ulverscroft Large Print Series:

THE CATALYST
THE SUNFARERS
THE RHINO STAYED FOR BREAKFAST

ROWENA LEE

THE RHINO STAYED FOR BREAKFAST

Complete and Unabridged

916.76

ULVERSCROFT

Leicester

First published 1958

First Large Print Edition
published September 1975
SBN 85456 371 7

© Marie Bartlett 1958

FOR
BILLY

This special large print edition is
made and printed in England for
F. A. Thorpe, Glenfield, Leicestershire

Part One

1

WHAT my husband and I knew about Kenya in June 1947 was very little indeed, but all the same to Kenya we were going. Our recent experiences in the Services had conditioned us to taking such leaps into the blue, firm in a blind faith that we would land on our feet. So when, after months of silence, during which we had abandoned all hope, the Colonial Office informed us that my husband had been accepted by the Kenya Government, that there was an appointment for him in the Kenya Public Works Department (he being a civil engineer) and that our passages were booked on the *Langola*, which was scheduled to sail in three weeks, we wasted no time asking ourselves whether or not we were doing the right thing in setting off to a country about which we were so ignorant.

As we saw it — here was adventure. We were elated at the prospect. Our horizons spun dizzily away beyond the equator and below the Southern Cross. My enthusiasm, though enormous, had physical limitations, however, for my baby was due the following January and I was suffering acutely from early malaise.

"Don't you know anything at all about Kenya?" our friends and relatives inquired. Since none of them knew either it seemed rather a pointless question. One or two did not even know where Kenya was in the first place, but everyone cast around obligingly for grains of enlightenment, coming back to tell us what they had gleaned.

A butcher down the road told my mother-in-law that he had a friend who was sent to East Africa during the war and ended up in a cannibal's stewpot. A friend said that her dentist told her that he had advised a couple who were setting off for Tanganyika to have all their teeth removed, sound ones included, for out there no dentist could come to the rescue if toothache occurred.

Along with the papers Billy, my husband, had to sign and return, the Colonial Office sent a little booklet. In it were set out all the tropical diseases we might get, with a passage of advice on how to treat snake-bite, and a footnote drawing attention to the fact that death within two and a half minutes could be expected from the bite of a black mamba. The booklet also stressed the fact that Kenya was one big, unfenced zoo, and wild game might be encountered anywhere at any time. A hatchet, a carving knife, cooking pots, water filter, mincing machine, tents and camping equipment were recommended as necessities. A rifle was indispensable and a horse's saddle might prove advantageous.

"The time has come," Billy said, when it was too late to change our minds, "to pool what little we know about Kenya." He got paper and pen and neatly set out a meagre list of facts.

(1) Kenya was about two and a half times the size of Great Britain. (2) Most of the country was raised several thousand feet above sea level. (3) There were snow-capped mountains with ice-fields and glaciers. (4) The Great Rift Valley split the colony from end to end. (5) There were hot, equatorial coastal belts, temperate Highlands, and hot, dry deserts to the north. (6) Up to the end of the nineteenth

4

century the whole area of Tanganyika Uganda and Kenya was known as "Darkest Africa" and had remained practically untouched by civilisation. (7) Tribes existed in Kenya — as elsewhere in East Africa — who belonged to pre-history, to cave-man times.

We studied the list doubtfully. The Colonial Office was unable to specify where exactly we were likely to be stationed. That we would learn when we arrived. In the meantime we could not discount the fact that our baby was due to be born in January.

"We'd better get to know all about that part, anyway," I said, and set about shopping for books on "How to Bring Babies into the World".

We had decided to spend our last fortnight on one big spree in London, and at that time a film called *Birth of a Baby* was attracting a great deal of attention. Expecting to glean useful hints, we went to see it.

The cinema was crowded and we were just able to find seats near one of the exits. Instead of usherettes, nurses lined the walls. It was a good film, helpful and informative, as well as encouraging, for it proclaimed that childbirth was a natural process, and that there was nothing to fear. The climax of the film was spoiled for me. A big man sitting on my right let out a small sigh and lolled sideways upon me, passing right out when the actual birth was shown on the screen. A couple of nurses were promptly on hand; but on looking round the cinema it was clear that several more good stout hearts had quailed and more men were being resuscitated in the aisles.

"Let's get out of here," Billy whispered urgently.

Once in the broad daylight I noticed his complexion had turned pale green. "You make me do the damnedest things," he muttered. But that was scarcely the point.

"Did you learn anything?" I demanded. "You might have to bring your own child into the world, you know."

"God forbid," he said, and hustled me off.

We set sail on a beautiful June evening. From ten degrees above the horizon the sunbeams rolled lavishly over earth and sea. The air was exceptionally clear, and beyond the green-blue of the sky was a diamond brightness, as if a great light shone from behind it. It was a difficult day on which to say good-bye to England.

There were many on that ship who were going away to start life afresh in a new land. The question in all our hearts was: would we ever return, would we ever see England again? With complicated emotions we watched the anchor come clanking up the ship's sides, the ropes and cables flung free and the gap widen between us and those who stood waving on the quayside.

Billy's hand found mine and held it hard. We did not leave the deck till England faded away in lavender mists. Left alone on that outward-bound ship in that strange lightlessness called dusk, we felt our first twinges of misgiving. What now, what now?"

The *Langola* was a part cargo-carrying, part passenger, ship. There were not more than seventy passengers, and in consequence no one attempted to organise fancy-dress dances, sports or deck games. Life was peaceful and there was ample time to get to know our fellow passengers.

A good proportion of them were like

ourselves — going out to take up appointments with the Governments of Kenya, Uganda or Tanganyika, with banks, or with the big mercantile firms. Some were Kenya settlers, returning from a holiday at Home. Some were new settlers. Many of the latter had served in Kenya during the war, fallen in love with the country, and were going back to buy land and farm or ranch. A few were destined for ports farther south — in Portuguese East Africa and South Africa.

After the austerity of British rationing, meal-times on the *Langola* were a treat. The food was good, well-cooked and plentiful. To a housewife accustomed to scurrying from one job to another in order to catch up with the day's routine, it was sheer heaven to relax in a deck-chair, feet up on the rail, to read or talk or just gaze upon the horizon.

I wasn't the only pregnant woman on board. There was the English wife of a learned Anglo-Indian doctor who was on her way to Uganda with him. She had never left Britain, and the future hung luridly before her, symbolised by her first glimpse of Africa: stark iron-bound ranges, like one gigantic wall, not covered by any visible vegetation but fantastically beautiful in their primeval mineral colours. "There's no sign of life," she kept saying, "just sand and rock and sea. Is that what is called Africa?" By eleven that same day the dust-devils stirred into activity. One o'clock found them rushing furiously over the beaches, forty to fifty feet in diameter, and seven to eight hundred feet tall.

"Wait till you get to Kenya," an old settler lady said. "Kenya is quite different." She told us that she had first gone out to Kenya when the Mombasa–Lake Victoria railway line was under construction. She and her husband had trekked 500 miles over mountains, through tsetse country, through mud and thorn and game lands. "Kenya nowadays is civilised compared to fifty years ago," she said.

There was Margery Livingstone-Diggins, daughter of Kenya pioneers, who was on her way back from buying farm machinery in Britain. Her baby was due about two or three months before mine and, though it was her first, she could not have been more casual. With sun-browned feet on the sun-heated ship's rail, she kept saying that there was nothing to having a baby.

"Particularly in Kenya, where the roads are a great help," she expounded. Several of her friends had been born in trucks or ox-drawn wagons. "The thing to do is to get thoroughly clued-up on how to produce your offspring. Also, at all times carry a suitcase in your vehicle with everything you're likely to need in case you have to stop somewhere and have the brat."

My friendship with Margery began then and there. She had a book of instructions which set out quite plainly the various steps in childbirth, how to detect the signs and how to deliver a baby. I studied this till I knew it by heart, but when I tried to coax Billy to take an interest in it as well, he refused point blank, saying that the illustrations were too revolting.

He concentrated on his Swahili text-book instead.

There were two women on board that ship who were to die within three months of our landing in Mombasa. One was middle-aged, arrogant and bossy. She was nasty to everyone, particularly to the younger women. One evening, finding me alone on the boat-deck, she made a point of telling me in gruesome detail of all the things that could go wrong when my baby came. "I'll be surprised if you live to see it," she said.

Afterwards Margery explained about her. "Don't mind the poor creature. She's had an operation for cancer. It was done too late. She doesn't know it, but she is returning to Kenya to die. Won't last six months."

The other was a quiet girl, with heavy hips, thick glasses and legs like milk bottles. She played snakes and ladders by herself. We thought she was proud and didn't care to mix with the rest of us. For hours on end she sat and stared at nothing. The only movement discernible on that impassive face was when her tongue went searching along her teeth.

She was well-connected, someone said. She was going out to marry a brilliant young man whose career was full of promise. She was rich.

Not three months after we arrived in Kenya we were shocked to learn of her death. It happened not a mile from where we lived. A gun her young husband was cleaning went off accidentally and blew away half her face.

To us, who had made journeys on other occasions through the Red Sea and the Mediterranean, the ports between Aden and London were already familiar. The voyage down the East Coast of Africa, from Cap Guardafui to Mombasa, was fresh ground and from this point on we eagerly looked landwards for a sight of our new country.

I remember those hot, still nights in the Red Sea. We carried our bedding up on the boat-deck and slept under the stars, because the heat in the cabins was suffocating.

By then it was early July, and a fiery breath flowed out of the deserts of Arabia and Africa. During the day the wood-work blistered on the ship, metal became too hot to touch, big tarpaulin troughs filled with water were slung above the deck rails in the hope of mitigating the heat. We sucked salt tablets till our tongues felt like pickled fish.

Then came the night, three o'clock in the morning to be precise, when the light-house beams of Cap Guardafui swept across the *Langola*'s bows. The Cap sits like a blister on an out-thrust thumb of land which is part British, part Italian Somaliland.

No sooner did we see the lighthouse than a wind rushed out upon us from the Indian Ocean, blew out the stars, and filled the sky with heavy-bellied cloud. Rounding the blister we were in the teeth of the monsoon winds. Down poured the rain, and the ship rushed up the slopes of sharply rising waves only to plunge down again, sucked into deep chasms. We grabbed our bedding and made our way to our cabin.

From now on we scanned the horizon to the west. When we passed a fleet of dhows skimming southwards, their lateen sails jauntily bobbing above the grey sea, we knew we were not far off.

"See those dhows," said Margery; "less than fifty years ago they were still carrying away slaves from Africa."

On the afternoon of the day before we arrived in Mombasa we saw the coast-line of Kenya, a black, fuzzy wall be-laboured by an attacking mass of cloud. The next morning we were steaming into Kilindini harbour. A heart-warming sight, I was informed later, but I missed it for I was bent over a basin being very sick in my cabin. Mornings were not my best time. However, every time I raised my head and took a peek out of the porthole I caught glimpses of coconut trees floating past, of baobabs and greenly swelling humps of land, of flamboyant trees in flower, of lateen sails folding like the wings of tired birds after their journey from the Persian Gulf, the Hadhramaut, Arabia or India.

Billy found me the moment I set foot on deck. "I have just had a talk with the Coast Agent. We're being sent to Nairobi. I am to work at P.W.D. Headquarters."

2

"THE train doesn't leave till four this afternoon," said Billy. "It's only ten o'clock now." There was ample time for exploring and I had recovered from my earlier bout of sickness.

Mombasa town is built upon an island and is the chief port, not only of Kenya, but of Uganda as well. Countries of Central Africa such as the Belgian Congo frequently make use of it in preference to the ports on the west coast. I expected to see a trading station consisting of a few white-washed mud-and-wattle huts upon a dusty clearing, for ever menaced by an encroaching equatorial forest. Instead we picked our way along pavements which flanked intriguing glass-fronted shops owned by Europeans, Indians and Arabs; saw wide streets enlivened by shining American cars; found up-to-date hotels, a cathedral and various churches, mosques and temples.

We hired a taxi driven by an Arab who

spoke excellent English. He rejoiced in showing off his knowledge of various places of interest as he drove us through the different quarters, English, Arab and Indian. The African quarter he dismissed contemptuously, the African being a dirty native and, by his standards, scarcely human. There were glimpses of green, well-kept lawns, bright-looking, well-designed bungalows, and everywhere a burgeoning of flamboyant, of purple and cherry bougainvillaea. We looked at the golf course and we admired the yacht club. We bought basketsful of mangoes, pineapples and bananas; we photographed the grim, sultry fortress of Fort Jesus, which stands as a monument to the Portuguese occupation of this part of the African coast. The fort is now a prison and its history is steeped in death and violence. Built at the close of the sixteenth century, it stood up to the wars between Portuguese and Arabs in their struggle for supremacy of the East African coast.

In 1631 the Portuguese Governor was stabbed to death while hearing Mass in the fort by one Yusuf bin Hasan, and his murder was taken as a signal for the massacre of all the Portuguese on Mombasa island. In 1696 the fort itself was besieged by Arabs. The defenders suffered from plague. Five hundred men arrived from Mozambique, which was then and still is the chief port of Portuguese East Africa, to reinforce the Portuguese garrison. For over eighteen months the siege dragged on, then, in December 1698, the Arabs stormed its walls, found eleven men and two women left alive, and promptly killed them off.

The relief fleet which came to the aid of the defenders arrived too late. They had crossed the Indian Ocean and were sent from Goa, in India. When they saw the Arabian flag flying above the fort they sailed back home. It was the red flag of the Sultan of Zanzibar which we photographed that bright morning, fluttering in the warm, salty wind.

We were driving along at a spanking pace up Azania Drive, with the turbulent, monsoon-tossed sea on one side, when in the vicinity of Ras Mzimba we began to pass a grove of ancient baobab trees.

"See those trees," our driver said, waving one arm and removing his eyes for several seconds at a time from the road, "Africans say they grow upside down. The branches under the ground, the roots in the air. Africans savage people. They don't know nothing."

Yet that was what the baobabs looked like.

"Those trees," continued our driver, "grow from bodies of Portuguese soldiers. One tree — one soldier."

Later we crossed over to the mainland and looked at Freetown. This is a settlement of freed slaves, founded in 1875. It was a luxuriant spot, green with foliage, full of coconut groves and banana plantations. Then we went down to the old harbour and looked at the dhows rocking sedately upon the satin waters, wings folded, while their Arabian crews swaggered through the villages with the air of buccaneers.

"Two-three hundred slave they take away in the old days," our driver said. "The slave stay down where you can't see. Some die and they are thrown to the sharks. When European made plenty trouble for the Arab slaver, then plenty trouble come also to the slave. When a dhow see a man-o'-war catching up with it, the captain say, 'Throw all slave overboard.' Nowadays the dhows make trade in carpets, in boritis poles, dates, dried fish, earthen pots. No more prosperity for the poor Arabs now."

"It was hard lines, though, on the poor Africans who used to be carried away to slavery," we said.

"Slave very good, you see," he told us earnestly. "African like to be slave. My father he has many slave. Then the European come and say, 'You liberate your slave.' My father say, 'O.K.' But his slave would not go."

"Didn't they want to be free?"

Our driver, who bore a striking resemblance to a hawk, chuckled knowingly. "Free? What for? A free slave must work to get money. No money, no food, no house, no dress. Now when he is a slave his master must give him food and a house and must look after him even if he does no work. African do not like work. He like plenty food, plenty womans and plenty sleep in the sun."

He felt that a homily was now called for: "European do not know one damn thing about Africa. He think African like hisself. Well, African is not like European. He is not like Arab and Indian. He is savage. He does not understand European law courts, European justice. European justice too long. African forgets at the end what has happened at the beginning of a case. He cannot understand why everyone sit and talk-talk-talk in a court of law.

"What he knows is what his chieftain do to him. Say he steal cattle or burn his neighbour's huts or carry off another man's wild honey. What happen? The Elders meet. They make trial by walking him over hot charcoal or suchlike. If he is guilty they beat him or they kill him. He understand that. Not this talk-talk-talk and everyone calm and not getting angry."

"How did the Arabs behave under such circumstances?"

"We catch and we beat. Good beating. Then all over. We do not kill, because slave means money. We beat. Finished. He understand. We understand. All friendly again."

We were well on time for our train.

Margery was on the platform and brought her husband over — she called him Diggy — and introduced him. Apparently the rains had got off to a good start but were tailing off too rapidly now. Margery, who lived just outside of Nairobi on a ten-acre plot of land, grew vegetables and corn. But it seemed that baboons had played havoc in the mealie patch and zebra had trampled down the vegetables.

"Makes you spit blood," she said. We were given her address and telephone number. We were to report to her without delay. "The pair of you are so green . . .! It just isn't true."

Billy and I had a coupé to ourselves and sharp on time the train started off. In the pioneering days railway stations were centres of social activity. The early settlers visited them regularly, not only to collect mail and parcels, but to see if any new faces had arrived in the colony and perhaps to exchange greetings with old friends. It was an era when everyone was known to everyone else. Train schedules were elastic, and obliging engine-drivers were known to pull up in rich game country so that passengers could put in a little shooting to relieve the tedium of the long journey.

Over the Makupa Causeway sped our train, plunging into the hinterland. Winding, twisting, doubling back upon themselves, the pair of gleaming lines kept on weaving over the rising ground. The lush coastal belt fell away. Trees dwindled from equatorial giants to tough, drought-riven specimens, squat, twisted and the colour of rhino hide, which the recent rains had persuaded into reluctant verdure. We saw no sign of human habitation.

However, as each of the far-flung stations was approached, we noticed a clustering of broken-down, mud-and-wattle huts about which squatted women, children, old men and young men, all silent and watchful, all more or less naked. The stations themselves were lonely oases in the wilderness. A few shy Africans would appear, spears in hand, lurking among the hibiscus bushes, staring hard at the alien monster in their midst. When the passengers descended to stretch their legs in the evening's cooling air, the Africans would melt away from view. But they would be there again when the Indian station-master came out and the guard waved his flag, to behold the fascinating spectacle of the train steaming away into the distance.

The few women we saw were clad chiefly in festoons of gleaming copper wire round their necks, arms and ankles. We learned later that all this copper wire had been pilfered from the Post and Telegraph Company of Kenya. Telegraph wires were in constant demand, and no sooner had a length of this irresistible source of adornment been fixed in position than it would mysteriously disappear again. Who stole it was seldom discovered, though the women in the neighbourhood would glitter forth with copper necklaces, bracelets and anklets soon after its disappearance.

Dusk comes swiftly upon the heels of twilight in tropical countries. Between the ordering and arriving of our sundowners, out went the twilight and on came the stars. Before us, on all sides, Africa opened up its gaping maw and our train bore us implacably into it. We popped our heads out of the windows. A circular horizon encompassed the night.

Down the corridor the car attendant, resplendent in gold-braided zouave and long white *kanzu*, came playing the dinner chimes. The whistle shrilled. Suddenly the rhythm of the wheels was loud, insistent, significant. That is it, this is it, this is it: an ominous reiteration. What were we doing here in Africa? Why had we come here? In that moment of panic what had seemed to me a glorious adventure became a piece of preposterous folly.

"Come on," Billy said gently. "We're in this together." As we made our way to the restaurant car, my fears abated. Suddenly I remembered I was hungry.

3

ARLY next morning the African railcar attendant woke us with cups of tea and some fresh fruit. Up went the blinds, down came the mosquito-mesh sashes. The Highland air, about 20°F. cooler than the coastal air, flowed into the coupé. We were puffing serenely over a treeless veldt, shot-silk, tawny-green in colour, and undulating to a horizon pushed out to the rims of the earth. The sun had not risen more than five degrees and in its beams every tussock of grass, every thornbush, trailed cauls of blue shadow. A herd of zebra, about forty strong, lifted nonchalant heads as we puffed by, their coats so bright and sleek that the long shadows trailing from them might have been birth membranes, freshly thrown. Before and behind us the single-track lines spun over the heaving veldt like a cobweb.

We had never seen country like this before or observed how the semi-spherical sky could sit as lightly as a soap-bubble upon a circular horizon. The high veldt of Kenya has been rightly described as one vast, unfenced zoo. We passed herds of wildebeest, deer, impala, and of gazelle, which took fright at our approach, if they happened to be too near the line, fleeing in agitation, scuts flipping, the black-and-white stripe along their flanks describing an arabesque of leaping parabolae. Three giraffe chased the train for about a quarter of a mile, but fell away in defeat.

A good proportion of the passengers alighted at Nairobi when we arrived at about half past nine that morning. Farewells were said all over again, and promises made to write, to visit, to keep in touch.

Billy's new chief met the train. He bade us welcome to Kenya and said that we were booked in for a week at the Queens Hotel. When that week expired we must find accommodation elsewhere, for Nairobi hotels, at that time, apart from long-established residents, refused to keep their guests for over seven days.

"The Colonial Office gave me to understand," said Billy, "that accommodation would be provided."

But of course there was a shocking housing shortage in Nairobi; people had to live where they could. We might put our names down for a house, but the list was long and the Housing Committee might not be able to find us a place for quite a little while.

"Priority is given to couples with families," said Billy's chief. "The more family the more certain you are of getting a roof over your head."

He himself had no family, and in consequence, though he had been some twenty years in the Service, he and his wife lived a nomadic existence, moving constantly from hotel to boarding-house, to rented rooms and again back to hotels.

Billy saw me and our luggage installed at the Queens, then went off with his chief to the Head Office of the Kenya Public Works Department. He advised me to lie down and rest, for the excitement had brought on a bout of morning sickness. One look out of my bedroom window at the fine buildings below, the traffic islands neatly planted with palms, the pavements lined with jacaranda trees and bushes of bougainvillaea brilliantly blooming in the crisp, cold, dry air, convinced me that the thing to do was to be out and about, exploring.

Walking down Delamere Avenue I came upon the *East African Standard* building. I made my way upstairs to the advertising department and put in an advertisement under "Accommodation Wanted".

The girl at the desk gave me a bored look. "This is the fifteenth since we opened this morning," she said. "Chum, you haven't a hope in hell of renting a house or bungalow. Might as well ask for the moon."

To cheer myself I strolled through Nairobi, noting the well-stocked shops, the multiplicity of vehicles on the roads which appeared to be of all types and makes, from Land Rovers and jeeps to trucks, country cars and gleaming American limousines. An African in much-patched European clothing stopped his bicycle beside me on the pavement, holding out a bunch of magnificent gladioli. Attached to the back of the bicycle was a large wicker basket, crammed with dahlias, daisies, antirrhinum, larkspur, red-hot pokers, carnations, lilies of various varieties, delphinium and love-in-the-mist.

"Here, take," he said, "only fifty cents. Take!"

Fifty cents was the equivalent to sixpence. There were about eight or nine stalks, each sporting four or five open blooms and numerous buds. I had never seen such large gladioli before. They looked artificial. The other flowers, too, were outsize. I learned later that a combination of high altitude and equatorial sun exaggerated the size of flowers and vegetables on the Kenya Highlands.

I bought the flowers, but I hadn't the nerve to pay only fifty cents for them. Back in Britain what would a bunch like that cost?

The man, a Kikuyu, took my shilling and began to fish out his purse to give back the change. I said the only Swahili word I knew at the time. *"Hapana"*. (No.) He gave me an incredulous glance and followed it up with a beaming smile. From that day to the time he was carried off in May 1953 to a detention camp where he was found to be one of the Mau Mau ringleaders, an oath administrator and a sworn killer, he remained a good friend of mine. He would always come over for a quiet talk whenever he saw me, and invariably I bought his flowers. I would be told a few titbits of gossip, then he would terminate the little exchange with: "All right. Now I go. *Kwa heri*." (*Kwa heri* means — till we meet again.)

The flowers in my arms made me feel so self-conscious that I crossed the road to a café. It was the hour when Nairobi office workers, visitors in from the surrounding farms and from up-country, housewives and indeed everyone else who happened to be in the city, took shelter from the sun, and drank coffee in the cool shade of coffee houses. I found a table with three vacant seats.

The café was run by Viennese Jews who had taken refuge in Kenya when Hitler was making things difficult for them in their native land. The coffee was good, the pastries and cakes better. My flowers lay on the table and I found it difficult to tear my enraptured gaze from them.

"Excuse me, may I have this seat?"

A young man with a deeply tanned complexion and bright blue eyes, holding a bulky parcel done up in leaves and newspapers, stood before me. He sat himself down and ordered himself a coffee. I moved the flowers out of his way.

In Kenya strangers talk to strangers, knowing no inhibition. Kenya is very large, the white population very small, and perhaps this has something to do with it. He crammed the bulky parcel under the third chair.

Over the coffee I learned that he owned a sisal plantation outside Nairobi. You couldn't miss it, he said, when you came in by train. In fact, I had noticed several sisal plantations alongside the railway line, the sharp-bladed rosettes which compose each bush sitting in prim rows that stretched for miles. Sisal planters were making good money, for sisal was a dollar earner.

"My place is too close to the Game Reserve," he said. "Can't keep the wild life out, and when in desperation we shoot down a few — lord, what a rumpus there is with the game wardens!" He indicated his parcel, which I understood contained the hide of a freshly skinned lion.

"Found that one in the labour lines last night. It was a constant visitor, carrying off the boys' cattle and goats.

Last night it killed one of my men. I had to shoot it."

But he looked apologetic. Obviously the dead lion weighed on his conscience.

That same day two other incidents occurred which brought home to me Kenya's schizophrenic nature.

On my way back to the Queens for lunch, I saw a procession bearing down on me from the opposite direction. Six young Masai *moran* (spearmen) and three gazelle-eyed young girls stalked along the pavement, heads held high, limbs free-swinging. The men wore crude hide slippers fastened by a single thong to their feet, and togas fastened on one shoulder over their naked bodies. The girls wore togas and aprons, plus plenty of crude ornaments in their ears, around their necks and ankles. The men wore their hair teased out with red ochre into an elaborate coiffure; the girls were shaven. The men walked jungle fashion in front of their womenfolk, holding their long spears in such a manner that, at the first hint of danger, the spears could leap forth with deadly accuracy. They had brought their vermin along with them too; their bodies, their garments, their skins, crawled thickly with flies, which rose up in swarms only to settle again in undetachable loyalty upon their hosts.

Seeing those Masai startled me as much as if I had come upon a procession of tigers strolling down Oxford Street.

The second incident happened in the middle of the night. We were in bed and asleep when the clatter of a dustbin lid falling upon the pavement under our window woke us up. There was strong moonlight. Immediately a yawling and a jibbering broke out — eerie, subhuman sounds. We went over to the window to investigate and saw three hyenas squabbling over the upturned contents of one of the hotel dustbins. Even as late as 1947 hyenas still walked down Nairobi streets on a scavenging expedition at nights. Ten years earlier, I was told, lions in Dela-mere Avenue were not considered unusual.

There was still the unsolved question of where to lay our heads. The sole hope of acquiring accommodation seemed to us to try booking in at Nairobi's chief hotels, a week in each, and work out a rotation system which would ensure we always had a roof.

I went round on the fourth morning of our stay at the Queens and made the necessary bookings at Torrs, the Norfolk, the New Stanley and the Avenue. I was much depressed. We were getting off to a poor start. The household linen, the pictures, our wood-carvings collected personally from various parts of the globe, the silver Billy's people had given us, all these objects which we longed to have around us in our new life looked as if they would be confined to a go-down for the rest of our three-year tour.

There came the morning on which we had to leave the Queens and move into the New Stanley. After breakfast, as I sat dejectedly flipping through months-old magazines in the lounge, a Mr. Robinson asked to see me.

He turned out to be an elderly gentleman who owned a bungalow within four miles of Nairobi post office. He and his wife had seen my advertisement and liked the look of it. Now here stood Mrs. Robinson, following up a hunch that we might be the right people to take care of their place while they went to South Africa for a holiday.

"That is, if you are still interested," he said modestly.

Was I interested! Already I was offering up little silent prayers of thanks. It was arranged that he should call for Billy and me in his T-Model Ford at half past four that evening. His wife would give us tea.

Mr. Robinson was then about sixty years of age. Forty years earlier he had trekked up to the Highlands with the aid of a bicycle. He was a genuine Kenya pioneer, and he still clung unconsciously to the attitude of the pioneer, finding the parking restrictions and the speed limits of latter-day Nairobi thoroughly irksome. In the old days, when Nairobi was a tented plain slung between the Ngong Hills and Don ya Sabuk, you just drove your vehicle to where you wanted to go and stopped when the spirit moved you.

No sooner had we climbed into his T-Model than we realised that he still drove his car as if such freedom from the rules of the road existed even today. Like a fire-engine the T-Model shot through the traffic, Mr. Robinson, loquacious and nonchalant, unaware of the sour looks and the scared shrieks of jay-walkers flying out before his wheels, and the squeal of tyres issuing from other vehicles madly jerking out of his way. Once off the tarmacadam, we bumped and bounced along corrugated roads, each corrugation iron-hard, five to six inches between ridge and trough and about eight inches apart. The roof of that T-Model was as much in need of padding as were its seats, for we travelled quite as much on our heads as on our behinds.

His bungalow rested at the top end of an avenue of grevillaea and eucalyptus, beyond an overgrown purple bougainvillaea which had climbed high up into a grevillaea, smothering it in a cascade of bloom. Mrs. Robinson, petite, white-haired and gentle, waited for us on the top step of the long verandah which ran the full length of her little stone bungalow.

While we stood on the gravel driveway, a little dazed, still feeling the bumpity-bump of those corrugations reverberating through our bodies, Mrs. Robinson came down to greet us with outstretched hands. "Welcome to Kenya," she said.

"Well, what do you think of it?" Mr.

Robinson demanded climbing out of the T-Model without opening a door.

House and garden gave an impression of peace and repose. It was an ideal spot in which to wait for the coming of one's baby. The air was pungent with the fragrance of cypress, of grevillaea and eucalyptus. Roses were in bloom. In a central flower-bed, seven-foot-high cacti grew, but Mrs. Robinson said that they rarely blossomed and then only at night. Before morning the flowers were already beginning to fade.

While we stood on the drive making small-talk I took stock of the bungalow. It was built on concrete piers, raised four feet above the ground. The space under the floor was partially screened by six-foot high geraniums which were in a riot of blossom. Where else in the world did geraniums grow so exuberantly? I shifted my gaze from a cluster and saw two beady, bright eyes looking hard at me. One minute they were there, the next they had gone, leaving me to speculate whether they belonged to a rat, a snake, a lizard or a blood-sucker.

It did not take long to go over the house,

which consisted of a large bedroom, a fair-sized drawing-room, a dining-room, a servery, a small kitchen with a Dover stove, and a bath and lavatory. Crockery and cutlery were being left for us to use and Mr. Robinson suggested that Billy should take the T-Model out occasionally. We had ordered a vehicle of our own and expected its delivery within a matter of days.

We had tea on the lawn. About an acre of garden ran out smoothly before us and then suddenly curved downwards very steeply, falling out of view. We were told that about two hundred feet below, a river flowed. During the dry months the river was no more than a meandering wetness of mud, but in the rains water bubbled and frothed through it in fine spate. However, we were not to bother about that river. No one ever went near it except the Africans.

"They hold meetings there," we were informed. "I sincerely hope they don't go in for *tembo* (beer) parties as well. The police don't approve of *tembo* parties."

What the Robinsons did not know, and what we as well as all the other Europeans who lived on either side of that river bank never suspected, was that there under our very noses Kikuyu were being rounded up, sedition was being pumped into them by trained Mau Mau leaders.

"Our servants want to be kept on," Mrs. Robinson said. "It's up to you, of course."

It seemed a good idea to keep on the Robinson's servants. Optimistically I thought to myself that there couldn't be much difference between servants in Africa and servants anywhere else. My mother had servants in her house; and during the war, when I was sent out to India, I found myself, like the rest of my fellow officers, in possession of a "bearer" a six-foot-four Pathan aged over sixty who had a predilection for pouring soup down the neck of any current boy friend who did not meet with his approval. Billy was one of the few who escaped this treatment.

"You will find the African servants a little different," I was told. "You need patience when dealing with them. They might seem obtuse, but remember that up to fifty years ago the African was a savage, he didn't even know what a wheel was. You'll find them ham-fisted. Hands have to be educated, and up to a few years ago the unsophisticated African was not accustomed to work which required any delicacy of touch. You must not be too indulgent. The African despises softness and indulgence. Be firm. Be just. Let them know they can trust you but cannot hoodwink you."

The Robinsons had two servants, Gushu and Wanyoki. When summoned and introduced, both men bowed politely. Both were dressed in clean white *kanzus*, and their faces had been freshly scrubbed. Their features were unmistakably negroid, with narrow foreheads, flat noses, prognathous jaws and receding chins. Wanyoki resembled a handsome ape, and Gushu, the head boy, was quite frighteningly ugly. His giraffe face on a human neck was enough to promote nightmares. With the dignity of bishops they heard Mr. Robinson out as he told them that they must be good boys and serve us well when we came to live there. They nodded solemnly, but their eyes were as bright and unreciprocating as an animal's, and it seemed to me that Gushu was sizing us up through his flaring nostrils.

The servants dismissed, Mrs. Robinson asked where we would stay for the next few weeks, until the time came to move into her bungalow. We confessed our predicament and how we had arranged to spend a week at each of the hotels.

"But that's preposterous!" she cried. "And you in your state! Why don't you try the Salisbury? I'm sure they'll have you both on a monthly basis."

So, when we got back to the hotel, we rang up the Salisbury and they agreed to have us straight away.

The next day I rang up Margery and told her of our good fortune. "A place to call our own, a car, servants and a telephone," I told her.

Had I done anything about fixing up a doctor and a nursing home? I hadn't, so Margery gave me the name of her doctor and advised me about the kind of nursing home to go to. In due course all arrangements were made. We could relax. This was only July as yet and the baby wasn't due till January. The doctor assured me that I was in excellent health, even the high altitude (Nairobi is over 5,500 feet above sea level) seemed to have no adverse effect.

On the fourteenth of August we moved into the Robinsons' bungalow. The new car was delivered. We refused to be unduly anxious about future accommodation. Perhaps by the end of six months the Government Housing Committee might furnish us with something.

"Don't depend on that," said Margery. "This being an agricultural country people know only one way to act. Biologically. It usually takes nine months between initial move and final results. In the meanwhile anything can happen. This, you must remember, is Kenya."

4

WE settled easily and comfortably into our new life. Billy came home every day to lunch. I slept in the afternoons, and though I did all the cooking there was yet plenty of time to read, write and to sew. Housekeeping in Kenya is free of drudgery.

In spite of my poor Swahili, I managed to make myself understood by the servants. It was to Gushu I issued instructions and he passed them on to Wanyoki, ordering the poor man about in a manner I would not have cared to use. But Wanyoki was a humble fellow and seemed not to resent being bossed about by Gushu.

One month passed. It was a period of trial, during which our servants treated us with polite wariness, taking careful stock. On our side we liked them, savages though they were. The holding back was entirely on their side until, after much sniffing out, they decided that we were not a bad lot as Europeans went, and a pleasant *rapprochement* was established.

I had been warned not to leave the pantry door open and to lock up all groceries, cigarettes, soap and so on. The African was not a thief, but he regarded his employer's property as his own, helping himself freely. I kept the keys, but decided to pay a ten per cent 'good will' on consumables such as tea, sugar, milk and so on to the men, so that the need to steal would not arise. When I made cake and baked bread they invariably got their share baked in a special tin for them. When I was cooking, Gushu was always on hand to help, but Wanyoki was kept at a distance, busy on the more menial tasks such as chopping firewood, scrubbing floors and blacking the Dover stove. In return for his assistance Gushu laid claim to the bowl in which the cake or bread was prepared. He would carry this off to his house, where, with no one to watch such undignified behaviour, he licked it clean.

Once Wanyoki raised his voice in protest, claiming a right to lick the bowl himself. There was a scuffle, which I pretended not to hear. Wanyoki received a bash on the head with the bowl, and the bowl had a large piece of enamel chipped off it.

"That Wanyoki dirty savage," Gushu piously informed me the next day.

Invariably I lost the keys, though I took every precaution to lock things up and hide the bunch away in some secret place calculated to baffle Gushu. But if I forgot, he knew. Solemnly I would be led to the spot, and patiently he'd remind me where and when I had secreted them. I would retrieve the keys feeling a certain loss of face; but with not so much as the twitch of a muscle would Gushu let me see that he was rocking with laughter inside himself.

The first real sign that our servants had taken a liking to us came one morning. I was sewing baby clothes on the verandah. Gushu squatted on the porch steps nearby, polishing brass. He seemed to like company while he worked. Up came the ugly giraffe face. "I spik Inglis," he announced.

This astonished me, for Mrs. Robinson was so sure the men did not understand a word of English. "Why didn't you say so in the first place?"

He put on his pious look. "European no like African spik Inglis."

"That's nonsense. I am delighted to hear it."

"Ah, but you not like other *memsaab*. You and *Bwana* no say 'African is dam savage.' You like us."

"Of course we like you. But you shouldn't have pretended that you couldn't speak English. All these days how you must have laughed at us!"

He shook his head gravely. "I no laugh at you."

"Swahili is supposed to be an easy language, but I just don't seem to be able to learn it."

"*Ndio*" (as you say), he agreed. "But you must learn. Swahili good to know in Africa." He came out with an idea he must have cherished for some days. "I teach *Memsaab* Swahili. You teach me Inglis. I want to read."

I agreed to this. I bought him an English Primer and for half an hour each day taught him to read. Within a month he was on his third book and I still floundered about unable to speak even kitchen Swahili.

Africans buy their wives with livestock. In choosing a wife, factors taken into account are health, strength, capacity for hard work, diligence and meekness. A man expects value for his livestock. His wife, or wives, must attend to his needs, ensuring that his life be pleasant and care-free. A *bibi*, or wife, must not only cook his food and bear his children, but she must dig and plant and harvest his *shamba*, milk his cows, fetch firewood from the forest, carry his burdens for him when he goes on a journey. I have seen a Kikuyu woman walking doggedly behind her husband, her body bent under a load of cooking pots, bedding, bundles and boxes, the leather strap which keeps these objects upon her back, biting into her shaven skull so that the imprint of it is there for life. If there is a child too young to walk, it sits perched on top of the load. Sight-lessly the mother plods on behind her lord and master, her eyes on the backs of his heels, her only clothing a filthy length of calico fastened over one shoulder.

But the husband walks upright. He glances about him, hailing friends, stopping to shake hands and pass the time of the day with *rafikis*. He jokes and laughs while his wife droops tiredly behind him, eyes dull and sunken into her head, her shaven skull glistening with beads of sweat.

Africans in Kenya estimate humanity by the standard of the male. A woman, not being male, is a lesser creature and a departure from the norm. *She* could be bought for a few cows. But who would think of selling a *man*?

Gushu had told me previously that he already owned a wife. He had bought one six months earlier and was thinking of buying another, but he found he hadn't the necessary will-power to save enough money for the bride-price. He and his *shillingi* were too easily parted. Would I help him to save to buy himself a second wife?

I got him a post office book and with much pride, month by month he noticed how the money mounted up.

One morning, when he was busy polishing the verandah boards, he announced, "I give for my wife twelve *debis* of beer, six cows and ten cats."

Up to now I was unaware of the actual market value of a bride. Intrigued as I was, I hesitated to show interest because he had a way of suspending work while he gossiped. There was yet a great deal of floor space unpolished.

"I say I give for my wife twelve *debis* beer, six cows, ten cats," he repeated loudly as if I were deaf.

The beer and the cattle I understood. "But why the cats?"

He rolled his giraffe eyes heavenwards. "Cats very good." I asked if the girl's people were bothered with rats.

He didn't know what a rat was, so I got out paper and pencil and drew one, which he recognised. "Ah, no, no! I not give rat. I give CAT." He fixed me with a look of sarcastic patience. Kindly he inquired if I didn't know what a cat was. I said I did and both drew a cat and miaowed like one.

He gasped in incredulous horror. "*Hapana!* I not give *paka*. I give CAT." Muttering to himself he broke into a fever of polishing.

It occurred to me then that perhaps he used the term cats for other members of the feline tribe, the commonest of the species in Kenya being the lion. Gushi came from lion country.

"Were the ten cats alive or dead?" I

tried to imagine Gushu with his giraffe face and his spindly legs capturing lions in order to buy himself a wife. The only weapon at his disposal would be the traditional Kikuyu bow-and-arrow.

"Alive," he said, sighing gustily with disappointment at so much stupidity. Viciously he dug into the tin of Mansion polish, scooped up a lump weighing about half a pound and smeared it thickly on the boards.

I did not reproach him for this wastefulness, for by now I was beginning to see him in the light of an intrepid lion-hunter. "Look here, Gushu. Did your cats make a noise like like this?"

I stuck fingers into my hair, fluffing it into the semblance of a mane, raised my head and roared. He gave thoughtful ear to the roars and tried out a few experimental ones himself. "*Hapana,*" he said sternly. "My cats give milk."

I couldn't see him milking ten lions. "What sort of a sound do your cats make?"

Deliberately he placed the polishing rag on the floor. He crouched on all fours, he nibbled grass, he bounded and he butted, bleating plaintively the while. Goats!

I told him the word was goat and not cat.

He shrugged. "Ah so? My wife good woman. She make for me a baby."

"How nice. Boy or girl?"

"No can tell. Baby not yet come." He gathered up cloths and polish and retreated hastily to the kitchen in case he was called upon to make further explanations.

We christened our new safari wagon "Cream Bun", because it was painted cream, and went off on weekend excursions in it. There was one good tarmacadam road at that time. It ran north of Nairobi, through the rich red-earth Kikuyu territory where flourishing *shambas* of mealies, wattle and vegetables grew, out to the edge of the escarpment. Then, snaking along the 8,000-foot wall of the escarpment, it dropped gradually to the floor of the Rift Valley, ran past Mount Longonot, the perfect cylindrical cone-shaped extinct volcano standing 9,111 feet above sea level, over undulating veldt where giraffe and zebra roamed, and where ostriches often lost their heads, got separated from the main flock and ended up pounding furiously on either side of a car for half a mile or so at a time.

A favourite weekend haunt of ours was the Lake Hotel on the banks of Lake Naivasha. Naivasha was not a big lake as lakes were reckoned in the Rift Valley; it stretched some twelve miles north to south by nine miles east to west, but the scenery was magnificent. Views of the western escarpment rising 10,000 to 12,000 feet above sea level were reflected in the mirror-clear water, and the spectacle of birds such as pelicans, cormorants and flamingoes wading along its shores, the flocks of wild-fowl and the sight of hippos snorting and snuffling in its more remote pools, were always an attraction.

We made friends with some people who farmed out in the Naivasha district and were often invited to stay with them. There were about seven hundred and fifty Europeans in the area and we invariably ran into someone one knew at the Sailing Club or the Polo Club.

Naivasha was only fifty miles from Nairobi. Some weekends we went still further afield: to Nakuru a hundred miles away and still on the good tarmacadam road which Italian prisoners-of-war had built: to lonely inns on the high Kinangop plateau 7,500 to 8,500 feet above sea level along bad dust-roads but amid scenery that was both splendid and a little frightening: to the cold, surly Aberdares, skirting black forests teeming with game, catching glimpses of the strikingly marked, long-haired colobus monkeys as they swung from branch to branch.

Of course, these excursions were not exactly prudent for one in my condition. But with so much to entice us out of our home we could not spend weekend after weekend merely roaming round the garden. However, I always took a suitcase with me in which I carried everything that might be needed for myself and my baby should I be caught unawares and far from home. By now, too, I had memorised every step in Margery's book of instructions and felt confident that should the necessity arise I could deal competently with the birth of my own baby.

On the other hand Billy took a very different view, but with much coaxing and arguing I got him round to my way of thinking.

Social life in Kenya is warm, gay and easy-going. In no time at all we had collected round us a pleasant circle of friends. We entertained and were entertained, entertainment taking the form of sundowners, dinner-parties and the occasional barbecue. Only once was I called upon to give a tea-party.

Some friends had a relative staying with them who did not approve of any but tea-parties. She thought our sundowners an excuse to consume too much alcohol and for the same reason deplored our dinner-parties. So to tea she came.

Our friends were beginning to feel rather depressed, for this relative of theirs was taking the joy out of their existence. For heaven's sake, they said, have us over to tea and mind you keep off the subjects of cinemas, hunting and suchlike.

For their sake I tried to make a good impression on this censorious relative. I baked a fine cake, made some excellent pastries, cut feather-weight sandwiches. Tea on the verandah was out of the question since a couple of squirrels were disturbing its peace by their uninhibited courtship.

Tea was to be served on the lawn. I sat my guests out on the cropped grass under a eucalyptus tree and waited till Gushu, summoned by the ringing of a bell, wheeled a tea-trolley out to us.

Previously I had given him a dainty lace tea-cosy, instructing him to be sure and put it on before he brought the meal.

Gushu enjoyed our parties as much as we did ourselves. He moved among our guests with the pontifical air of a bishop in his long white *kanzu* and his red *zouave*. He also liked to gobble up leftovers once out of range of vision and before Wanyoki could get at them.

The African loves to adorn himself with European clothing. Cast-offs are picked up and treasured. On that occasion I remember, when I rang the bell and Gushu appeared trundling the tea-trolley before him, he not only sported the tea-cosy, which was perched on his head, but had put on my discarded maternity corset *over* his *kanzu*.

5

GUSHU obtained permission to bring his wife to Nairobi. It was her first excursion out of the Reserve, where she had lived all her life, so she had seen few white people and never worked in a city or a town.

European houses in Kenya have separate servants' quarters, built with the same materials used in the main house. The Robinsons' servants' quarters had one good-sized room which Gushu and Wanyoki shared, a small kitchen and fireplace, a shower and a lavatory. The presence of a woman, I feared, might complicate existing arrangements, but I didn't care to question Gushu as to how he was going to get over these difficulties: in such cases it's best not to know.

The wife arrived in due course, but Gushu did not mention her presence. I was surprised one morning to see her, as I strolled round the garden after breakfast gathering flowers for the vases. She sat in the dust under a hibiscus hedge behind the servants' quarters, as immobile as a lizard in the sun, her spindly legs stuck straight out in front of her, her hands idle in her lap. Her complexion was reddish-brown and not black like Gushu's. She could not have been more than sixteen or seventeen years of age, but already youth had had its brief flaring and was gone; I saw only its ashes in the deep-sunk, corpse-like eyes when her glance flickered up at me.

I said *"Jambo"* and stopped to pass the time of day. She did not appear to have heard. The only acknowledgement of my presence was a nervous shifting in the dust.

She was far advanced in pregnancy and her lips and ankles were swollen. Though so young, the indentation left by her leather carrying-strap was already clearly marked across her shaven skull. Her ear-lobes had been pierced and the holes stretched till each held a circular piece of soft wood, three inches in diameter. I tried again to evoke some spark of response, but she just sat there like a dumb animal. Her only garment was a verminous piece of *Americani* fastened with a knot over one shoulder and her skin was thickly patterned with dirt. Though flies supped unabashed at the corners of her eyes she did not appear to feel them.

I hurried back to the house. Gushu squatted in the sun on the back verandah, complacently burping over the remains of a tomato and kidney pie which he had swallowed without sharing it with either his wife or Wanyoki. Courteously he rose.

"Why didn't you tell me your *bibi* was here?"

He shrugged. The African's attitude to women is anything but praiseworthy. "She come," he said indifferently.

"You should have brought her over to see me. She looks a very nice girl and she is very young."

"Ah no," he said piously, "she dirty savage."

"How dare you call her that!"

He sulked. After all, only Europeans were supposed to refer to Africans as dirty savages. "*Memsaab*, she dirty. I do not want you to see her."

"There's plenty of water in the bathroom."

"I have no soap."

58

There was always a cake of soap left in the kitchen for the servants' use. They were supposed to wash their hands with it when they came into the house, but I knew they used it to wash their clothes, and certainly carried it off to use when they bathed, for a cake seldom lasted as long as two days. "She can use the kitchen soap," I said.

"She no have clothes," he told me repressively, fearing no doubt that I planned to give his *bibi* ideas above her station.

"What's wrong with washing what she already has ?"

"*Memsaab*, if she take off the *Americani* she have nothing on."

"Is that filthy rag all she possesses ?"

He was being put in the wrong and didn't like it. I asked him why he did not buy his wife a dress, and he promptly said he had no money to do so. I reminded him of the tie he had bought three days ago with the picture of a can-can dancer on it and for which he had paid fifteen shillings.

"You can take some money out of your post office book," I suggested.

Up went his hands in incredulous horror. "That money for my new wife. Her father ask big bride-price."

I decided to give his *bibi* one of my own maternity gowns, for I had more than I could use. He promptly brightened up. The next question was: had he made any provision for the baby that was coming? I didn't think under the circumstances that baby clothes had even been thought of — I was right.

He looked at me as if I were going out of my mind. "*Memsaab*," he said patiently, "baby might die. *Bibi* might die. Must wait an' see first."

It was no use arguing. I went in and got out a blue flowered skirt and a matching smock. Gushu grabbed it, went over it carefully. I saw what was passing in his mind. In the bazaar that dress would fetch a good price.

"I expect your *bibi* to be wearing that dress when she comes to see me in half an hour's time," I said.

When eventually the girl was led to the bottom of the verandah steps she looked comely and attractive. Pride struggled with bashfulness and she could barely bring herself to look above ground level. Gushu was in high spirits.

"Now she look like *Memsaab*," he giggled.

"When is the *toto* due?" I asked. But neither Gushu nor his *bibi* knew. Babies came when they came.

"Where will she have her *toto*? In a Nairobi hospital or in the Reserve?"

Gushu thought this so funny that he translated it into the Kikuyu dialect, and his *bibi* made a snorting noise which signified that even she was amused. "African no go to hospital, *Memsaab*," Gushu explained tolerantly.

The Robinsons had mentioned the popularity of the river as a meeting-place among the servants of the neighbourhood, so I thought nothing more about it when, every day, after lunch, batches of Africans followed each other in single file down the footpath which led to the unseen river below. Gushu and Wanyoki always went to the river of an afternoon and when I asked Gushu what they did there he said they talked. They talked of many things, he said.

This seemed innocent enough to me. . . .

Every afternoon I retired to my room and enjoyed a good hour or two's siesta. What I did not know was that Gushu used to lock me in the house and take the key with him. Before I was awake, the servants would have returned, the doors opened and the tea laid on the verandah. It was not until Gushu's *bibi* had been with us for three weeks that I realised I was being locked in.

One afternoon I had no sooner dozed off than there came a knocking on the window. It was the *bibi*. Her face was grey, her eyes had retreated deeper into their sockets, her skin glistened with sweat. She crouched on the grass like a stricken animal, looking up at me with an expression that had gone beyond fear and despair. The agony in that glance was terrible to see.

I dressed and made for the telephone. I had to seek the operator's advice before I could locate the right authority to approach in such an emergency. The African who eventually took my call appeared to be singularly detached. I bullied and scolded, seeing again the *bibi*'s tortured glance. The man went to fetch someone else and eventually it was arranged that an ambulance should call over at once.

When I tried to get out of the house I discovered that all the doors were locked. As the windows were securely curtained with burglar-proof steel mesh, an exit through them was out of the question. Fortunately I remembered the little square above the washbasin in the bathroom, which for some unknown reason had no mesh. When I tried this window I found that I fitted neatly into it, with hardly an inch to spare. Never did round peg fit more opportunely into square hole. I dropped safely among the geraniums.

The *bibi* still crouched under my window. For want of anything better to do, I sat myself on the grass beside her and waited till the ambulance turned up.

There are many tribes in Kenya who circumcise their girls at the age of puberty. The rites are performed with ceremony and celebration and the operation is carried out by an aged crone using a piece of broken glass or the sharp edge of a rock. Jomo Kenyatta, the Kikuyu who had given his tribe an explicit blueprint for Mau Mau terrorism, protested at his trial that the circumcision of girls was a "beautiful thing". Those girls who did not die of septicaemia after the operation lived to bear their children in intensified agony and at great risk to their lives.

The ambulance arrived and the *bibi* was removed to hospital, where that same night she gave birth to a ten-pound boy.

When Gushu came back home he showed mild surprise on learning what had happened. "Oh so!" he said, nodding. Why she didn't sit in his room and have the baby there he couldn't understand.

"How dare you lock me up in the house?" I demanded. "I had to climb through the bathroom window to get out."

He was sorry about this. "*Memsaab*, I lock door because you sleep. You sleep like a child and you don't know anything. Plenty bad man come and go through this *shamba*."

Margery's baby arrived in due course. We went to visit her at the nursing home and found her sitting up in bed issuing instructions to two of her *shamba* boys who had been summoned expressly for the purpose. Margery's mother came into the room, carrying a bonny baby girl, proudly showing her off, while Margery herself adopted a nonchalant attitude.

"Not a bad brat," she informed us.

"Came without any trouble. Of course the road helped. When the pains started I made Diggy take me out beyond Dagoretti. More pot-holes and corrugations on it to the square yard than on any other Kenya road. You must try it when your time comes."

My baby was not due till the middle of January 1948, and I was still making week-end trips out into the blue with Billy. The only concession I made to pregnancy was to take along the suitcase packed with all I might need in an emergency, a primus stove and a can of clean water. It seemed that the arrival of babies always called for plenty of hot water.

On Sunday the 7th of December, after hearing an early Mass, Billy and I set out for a delightful inn seventy or eighty miles away from Nairobi, tucked away in the high folds of the Aberdares. The weather was perfect, with clear blue skies and a dancing sparkle in the air. It had rained the previous night and the earth smelled fresh. The vegetation had been washed clean of dust. Cobwebs, five to six feet in diameter, spanned the bushes, beaded with flashing drops of moisture.

But the road, once we turned off the tarmac, was not too good. Erosion holes, a foot to eighteen inches deep, pitted the surface. Where there were no holes there were corrugations. In the higher reaches of the mountains, when we were nearing the bamboo forests about 9,000 feet above sea level, recent rains had scoured out great weals that caught at the car wheels, wrenching them out of alignment.

But when we reached the lovely inn the journey was forgotten. We lunched. We strolled over the well-turfed lawns. We took snapshots. I felt strange new sensations beset me, but these I dismissed, for who doesn't feel such sensations when pregnant?

Later that evening came a definite and unmistakable sign. Quite clearly I had reached stage eight in Margery's instructions.

"We'd better go back home," I confided to Billy. "I believe we're about to become parents."

Back then to Nairobi we raced, the Cream Bun rising magnificently to potholes, corrugations and erosion weals. Her chassis was permanently twisted and her springs damaged, her sump was all but wrenched off, but she never stopped once. I was enthroned at the back of the vehicle making ready for the birth of my child. I must have been in agony, but there was so much else to do I had little time to think about it.

Billy was all but speechless. The thing he had dreaded most seemed about to happen to him. He could hardly find voice to call out the mileage when I asked him from time to time. "Fifty miles." . . . "Forty miles." . . . "Only thirty now. How are you doing?"

When the wide sky gave way to eucalyptus trees, and these again to grevillaea and jacaranda, I knew Nairobi had arrived. Tiled roofs flew against the stars, neon lights flashed, street lamps ran dot and carry. "Here we are," said Billy.

My baby arrived within eighteen minutes of reaching the nursing home. We called him Ralph. Brief and no fuss. Ralph.

Friends came. My room filled with flowers. Gushu brought his wife and *toto* and stayed half an hour gossiping, though the nurses were not particularly pleased to see him squatting there in my aseptic surroundings. His *bibi* modestly turned away and fed her infant and Gushu inserted a fifty-cent piece into Ralph's clenched fist.

Our tenure of the Robinson house was drawing to a close and while I lay in the nursing home Billy began to hunt round for accommodation for us. The Government Housing Committee said again they would see what they could do but promised nothing. We advertised and answered advertisements. Estate agents had nothing to offer.

Soon we were considering the merits of taking to tents. The Government issued good living tents to its employees and we would certainly not have been the first young couple to live under canvas in Kenya. Billy made inquiries. Tents were available as well as camping equipment, but he was advised against camping on the west side of Nairobi, for though the pitches were good, the area was in the neighbourhood of the Game Reserve and National Park. A fellow P.W.D. official who had camped out there said that he and his wife were kept awake night after night by lions sniffing round under the canvas.

"Out Thika way would be better," we

were told. "There it's only leopards."

Three days before I was due to leave the nursing home Billy was offered a place some ten miles out of Nairobi, Thika way. He promptly went to inspect it. The accommodation turned out to be not a full-grown house but the nucleus of one. It consisted of two rooms held apart by an open verandah eight feet long and four feet deep. Behind the verandah was a tiny room with a wooden table and some old chipped enamel washbasins and jugs. The bath was shaped like a coffin and made of zinc. Bathing water came from the river on donkey-back, carried in tin *debis*. Drinking-water had to be fetched from Nairobi.

There was no kitchen, but three sheets of corrugated iron obligingly leant-to. The roof was weighted down with good-sized boulders, for the wind upon these flat, high plateaux moves with considerable velocity. Another sheet of corrugated iron supported on poles at the opposite side of the nucleus formed an overhead protection for a vehicle.

"It isn't much," Billy said, "but it's somewhere."

We took it, preferring to live under a

roof than under canvas, agreeing with our friends who came round to advise us, that bricks and mortar could not be carried off on the back of a charging rhino, as was the way with the poles, rope and canvas. One had to look at the matter from all angles.

The Nucleus stood on twenty acres or so of veldt. The land was almost flat. Harsh, sharp-edged grass grew above knee-height upon it, rolling out to a cinnamon-tinted horizon. When I first saw this hunk of veldt the grass was turning from green to tawny gold, for the rains had been disappointing and the long, dry season was on its way.

To get to the Nucleus we had to leave the tarmacadam road five or six miles from Nairobi, and then cut across the veldt along a dust track. The track was shared by our neighbours to the west who lived in an even more remote region than ourselves and whose distant chimney-pots we could barely make out beyond the shimmering dust haze. There were neighbours to the south as well, people called Timber-Dicks, but their homestead was out of sight, being some eight or ten miles away.

Billy was not able to come home to lunch

after we moved into the Nucleus. "I don't like the idea of leaving you and baby on your own in this wilderness all day," he said. "It looks like the abomination of desolation. Anything could happen and I wouldn't know until I got back in the evening."

But we hadn't much choice and I felt there was nothing to be gained by taking a gloomy view. The Robinsons arrived and we handed over their house, all duly swept and garnished and in a creditably sparkling condition. The only hitch in the hand-over was Gushu. He refused point-blank to return to the Robinsons and insisted on following us. We did not like to keep him because he was not really our servant at all. But Mrs. Robinson pointed out that he would be no good to her if he wanted to be elsewhere.

"We must give this contraption a name," Billy said as he pulled up the Cream Bun a little way along the drive the better to view our new abode. All our belongings were on board and my Ralph snuggled into his carry-cot full of milk and virtue. The Nucleus had the appearance of a wart growing out of the unending veldt.

We christened it "*Shenzi Ville*", *shenzi* being the Swahili word for barbarous, un-civilised, native and makeshift. "We could all be done to death out here," said Billy, whose views tend towards the pessimistic, "and no one would be any the wiser."

6

THE dust track which ran between Shenzi Ville and the main road was no worse than other Kenya roads Its corrugations were as iron-hard, its erosion scars as erratic. Only in its pot-holes could it lay any claim to distinction. These had exceptionally sharp rims, and were deep enough for a man to lie curled up inside unharmed if a vehicle, straddling the hole, drove over it. Persistently an ant bear dug fresh entrances and exits to his sub-terranean burrow along the surface of the track. The ground being so hard, all that digging must have expended much of the creature's energy. So as not to cause it un-necessary inconvenience, Billy would make a detour round these holes, wearing out new sections of the veldt, a manoeuvre we described as "blazing new tracks in Africa".

Wherever we went Ralph went with us, curled up in a basket, a mosquito-net draped over him. Gushu came along too and kept an eye on Ralph, ready to summon us should we be needed. But Ralph had a wonderful capacity for sleep. When awake he would study his fingers with much concentration. He preferred orange juice to milk, sucking enthusiastically at the teat when there was orange juice in the bottle and making wry faces if there was milk.

Returning home at nights from the cinema or after dining with friends, we often surprised the ant bear plodding steadfastly along, snout to the ground, long hairless tail dragging in the dust. The glare of the car lights confused him. He would panic forward, not knowing whether to turn left or right, constantly trying to do both. We would drive on, chasing him and teasing him, then, when we thought he had had enough, we'd switch off the lights, allowing him to make his getaway in peace. There were other creatures that we caught in the lamp-beams. Hare mostly, occasionally a herd of frantic bush-buck, sometimes that minute deer which is called dik-dik, snakes, nocturnal birds like the night-jar, wild cats, mongooses and rats. Though the district had a bad name for leopards we met only one face to face.

The animal had killed and dragged his victim into the fork of a tree. There were very few clumps of trees in the area, and those that existed were man-planted. Billy had caught a glimpse of two red embers glowing some ten feet above the ground. He thought it was a wildcat and decided to give it a shock.

Switching off the lights, he crept forward, easing the Cream Bun in and out of pot-holes, until he came under the glowing eyes. Then switching on all lights, including the powerful spotlight, he blew a fanfare on his horn.

I think both of us were more surprised than the leopard at what followed. The animal leapt forward and landed squarely on the bonnet. For a second or two he teetered there, his claws slithering on the smooth surface. Then suddenly he wasn't there. We caught a fleeting glimpse of him bounding away into the grass.

Sometimes the stillness of the veldt would be punctuated by the sound of distant rifle-fire. Our Neighbour-to-the-West explained that we were not to worry when we heard it. His mother wanted a leopard-skin coat and he was collecting one for her. "Some of the pelts are ruined by claw marks and teeth marks," he complained. "I wish these brutes didn't scrap so much. The last three were useless."

We called on them and they called on us. Whenever they drove past Shenzi Ville they would thump a greeting on the horn, and Gushu had instructions to return the compliment by beating on an old brass gong. As their vehicle was invariably enclosed in a cocoon of dust they could not see us, nor we them, so waving hands was useless.

With no trees in the immediate vicinity of Shenzi Ville to hold the sky off, we felt curiously exposed. At nights the stars leaned down and should a cloud appear I felt I had only to rise on tip-toe and stretch up my arms to tickle its underside. Nor had anyone warned us that Mount Kenya was visible from Shenzi Ville.

On the morning after we moved in, I went out on to the verandah a few minutes after sunrise to take a good look around me. This was easily done, for nothing obscured the vision between me and the horizon. The previous day the sky above the horizon had been cinnamon-tinted with suspended dust. But heavy dewfalls had laid the dust, the air was clean and there rose against the sky the majestic shape of Mount Kenya, its snows the colour of strawberry ice cream, its glaciers glittering.

Billy joined me on the verandah. Together we watched the progress of the sun and how the colours in the sky changed from turquoise and salmon-pink and pale ale to lighter, brighter colours until all colour was bleached out in an intensity of light so splendid that the human eye found it hard to endure.

We had had an uncomfortable night. The bedroom windows had no glass in them. The few wooden bars over each were to discourage the leopards. The windows being small, the room was dark and dank. In the rains, mildew must have flourished upon the walls, for now, even in the dry season, large grey patches remained. The furniture must have been bought in the last century, when they built solidly and heavily. Also, every stick of it must have travelled the 320 miles from the coast to Shenzi Ville dragged along behind an ox wagon. Upon the large double bed was marked the history of prolonged conjugal non-co-operation. A ridge ran down the middle and the mattress sloped steeply to the sides. It was all we could do that first night to keep ourselves from sliding off. The next night we slept on camp-beds, leaving the double bed to steam away on its own like an altar deprived of sacrifice.

"There's one other little matter," said Billy. He said it the previous afternoon when we had just arrived.

He led me round the house. Ten strides and we were at the back, looking past the squatters' *shamba* across still more veldt to the dark crests of trees which marked the passage of a small river. While we stood there blinking against the pulverising glare, feeling our eyeballs throbbing like dying protoplasm, we noticed a naked African come up from the river, driving a donkey before him. He was in no hurry. He had bathed and was now drying off in the sun. His voice, raised in tuneless ululations, carried clearly. The length of *Americani* which was his normal garment, now hanging round the donkey's neck while he dried, hit back a white spot of glare in the consuming light.

I noticed a wooden hut half-concealed

behind a short length of fence upon which straggled a passion-fruit creeper. It stood about a hundred and fifty yards from the house, and the same distance to the right of the squatters' *shamba*. Obviously it had no connection with the squatters.

"That," Billy informed me, "is the house-of-humble-purpose. The pit is at least fifteen feet deep and the wooden box harbours, lizards, earwigs, spiders and cockroaches. I have seen for myself."

We were expected to do our cooking upon two charcoal-burning braziers and an old oil-stove which smoked prodigiously but gave out so little heat it was almost impossible to boil a kettle of water. We still had our primus stove with us and on it I cooked all our meals, sterilised Ralph's bottles and prepared his food. Bathing water was heated in *debis* over three large stones and a wood fire in the open.

"You are going to have a tough job," Billy said. "Think you feel equal to it?"

"It won't be for long. The Government is bound to allocate a house to us sooner or later."

With the property went a family of squatters. The head squatter was a Kikuyu named Mwangi, described to us as "an unspoiled and unsophisticated African of the old school". He was thin, elderly, and frantically ugly. He owned many wives, each of whom lived in a round, windowless *rondavel* which looked to me like a toadstool. They all got on very well. I never saw any of them do a hand's turn beyond cooking *posho* and curry-combing each other's thick, woolly hair in the sun. Mwangi and all his wives made it clear to us that we were unwelcome, and that our presence was strongly resented. Any efforts on our part to be friendly proved of no avail.

There were no servants' quarters. Our servants, Gushu and a new *shamba* boy called Kimani, had to make do with a *rondavel* in the squatters' *shamba*. I feared this arrangement might not work, but as they were all of the same tribe, it appeared to go off very well. In fact the very next day after we moved in I saw Mwangi's third-but-youngest wife and the fourth carrying bowls of steaming *posho* into our servants' *rondavel*. They stayed with the boys for an hour or so.

"Why does Mwangi dislike us so?" I

asked Gushu. The man went out of his way to be horrid, gibbering whenever he saw us, gesticulating, making remarks to his wives which caused them to laugh uproariously.

"He dirty savage," Gushu said. "*Memsaab* no care."

The veldt flowed like a lake to the very steps of the verandah. For a drive we had only the track worn out by the coming and going of vehicles. From a distance the veldt had a smooth appearance, but at close quarters the kind of veldt which surrounded us consisted of tussocks of sabre-sharp grass, then withering to straw, each tussock about three feet in diameter and surrounded by short, tough skeletons of weeds. When I tried to pick my way through the grass I found that the blades slit the skin of my legs till they bled freely.

The veldt invariably presented a deserted appearance. But every time I attempted to take a little walk through it I discovered that all kinds of creatures had made their homes among the tussocks. Several times bushbuck sprang up and galloped away at my approach. Birds would rise in panic, beating their wings in my face. Fury little mammals like rats, mongooses or weasels would scamper out of sight. It was the sight of a serpent, strikingly patterned in black and orange, watching me with un-winking eyes, which put a stop to my wanderings into the bush.

As the weeks went by and no news of a house came, we decided to settle in at Shenzi Ville and make ourselves more comfortable. Our wireless set, a powerful one purchased in Britain, was of no use to us because there was no electricity, so we bought a small portable battery set. Then we decided to clear away some of the veldt.

We hired African labour and, working along with them in the weekends, Billy and I soon had a good-sized patch of cleared ground around the house. The soil was rich and red, but this was no time to plant a garden, for it was the dry season and the soil so friable that every puff of wind sent it flying up in clouds. We put down a bad-minton court and every evening, if the wind was not too strong, played a few sets.

"This is no place for a baby," Billy said one night as we lay in our camp-beds listening to a leopard push his way into the little bathroom and drink the water in the zinc bath. Next morning we found his foot-prints all over the floor.

Every night we shook our pillows, hunted under beds, and poked behind boxes in search of snakes. We could never keep them out. How they came in I never knew, for I watched the bedroom door constantly. One morning Billy groped for his slippers and felt something stone cold and alive moving under his instep. He removed his foot just in time. It was a puff-adder.

Margery called on us. "It could be worse," she said cheerfully. "My folks started with mud-and-wattle."

I felt a proprietorial pride in our wilderness. "Leopards prowl about at night and drink our bathwater."

"With us it used to be lions," she said reminiscently.

"Hyenas squabble over our garbage cans."

"Put down plenty of pepper. They don't like it."

As if to prove how intimately we lived with nature, a greater bustard at that moment flapped over the clearing and alighted not fifteen feet from us. It carried a wriggling snake in its beak. "Some people eat them," Margery said, indicating the bird. "For myself I prefer francolin."

I turned away so as not to see the bird, which stood about three feet high, consume the snake.

"Watch out for mamba," Margery said. "This place must crawl with them." The mamba is the most deadly snake in the world. By that time I had become so snake-conscious that I could not bear to let Raph out of my sight. I carried him around in his basket wherever I went.

"Why don't you pop the brat into the Lady Northy?" Margery inquired. "They may be a little expensive, but they have a trained staff of nurses to look after babies. He'll be quite safe there."

We hadn't even heard of the Lady Northy, but the next day I wrote to the matron. The reply came a few days later. All letters were delivered to Billy's office, for up to the time I left Kenya in August 1954 there was no form of postal delivery. The matron said she would gladly have Ralph, but he must wait seven weeks, for until then she had no vacancy.

Mwangi's youngest wife was a girl of about fourteen, unformed and still growing. He never bothered to clothe her. A scrap of verminous goat-skin draped apron-wise about her little body was her only garment. Gushu informed me that Mwangi had got her cheap and that she was a dirty savage.

For weeks I watched that child. She was made to fetch and carry for the others. It was she who was sent into the snake-ridden veldt to gather twigs for the fire. Her thin little body could be seen at all hours of the day staggering up from the river-bank carrying *debis* of water.

I cut down one of my dresses and altered it to fit her. I found a silk scarf, pressed it and put it on top of the dress. Then I told Gushu to fetch the girl. To send the dress to her might have tempted one of the other wives to steal it. Or Mwangi himself might have confiscated it to sell in the bazaars.

When the girl was brought before me, her goat-skin garment flapping in the high, cold wind of the veldt, goose-pimples prickling on her skin, I saw she was so very dirty that her flesh, coated with the red friable soil of the veldt, had thickened into a hide.

I showed her the dress and the scarf and

asked her, through Gushu, if she would care to have them. She nodded eagerly. I told her they were hers on one condition. I would give her a piece of soap and a towel; she must go down to the river and wash herself clean.

Eyes sparkling she agreed.

A little later a black and comely creature, wearing her handspan of apron, stood on the verandah steps. I could hardly recognise Mwangi's youngest wife. I held out the dress and scarf. She snatched at them. The dress was a puzzle. How could she get into it? She had never worn such a garment before. Leaving Gushu to instruct her, I went indoors.

Five minutes later Gushu knocked on the door. "She is ready," he said. I went out to see the transformation and was delighted. Mwangi's youngest wife took herself off to the *rondavels* in great pride. When she went among the other wives and they crowded round to inspect, she dodged out of reach of their clutching hands, pulling her skirts to herself with great disdain.

That same day Mwangi himself came over to thank me. This was more than I expected. He brought along a few eggs and when I offered to buy them he would have none of it. This was a social call. Gushu squatted on the verandah step alongside him and we all drank cups of very sweet tea and talked of many things.

From that day onwards his attitude to us changed. He ranged himself on our side. We were his *rafikis*. That he still thought us green and ignorant he made abundantly clear, but in a tolerant, friendly way. When next we attempted to go for a walk through the veldt, he came out, scolded us, asked us if we wanted to be bitten by mambas, and ordered us back to the house. We took this in good part, thanked him for warning us and returned to play a game of badminton instead.

He liked to boss people around, and as we had now been taken under his wing he never hesitated to tell us what to do. As he cackled and bustled around his own *rondavels* so he was soon cackling and bustling round us. But he had his spells of idleness too. He would spend long periods of time squatting at the entrance of his own *rondavel*, staring blindly into the sun. All the same he missed nothing.

It did not take him long to realise that

we went in shrinking terror of using the little house. His tilted slits of eyes would watch us as we picked our way gingerly over the rough grass, carrying a heavy walking-stick and a good powerful torch. The stick was for knocking the sides of the box. The torch was for making sure that having done so, no more livestock remained concealed inside the box but had fallen into the pit. When good relations between us were established, Mwangi took upon himself the rôle of beater-of-the-box. No sooner had those glittering slits of eyes noticed that either Billy or I was making for the little house, than out he'd come, carrying a cudgel. He would be in the hut before us, belabouring the box till we feared he would break it up. Then, having made clear what was happening to anyone within a mile, he would reappear, looking solemn and responsible.

"You may go in now," he would say, standing by in case his presence was needed. Nothing could persuade him to give up this performance. He dismissed all our protests and continued to act as beater-of-the-box until the day we left.

One Saturday morning when Billy was

inside the little house and was as usual playing his torch around the inside of the box, a movement in the pit caught his eye. He shone the torch down and saw a six- to seven-foot-long black mamba going round and round the circumference of the pit, raising itself a foot or two at a time, trying to climb upwards, but defeated by the smooth vertical walls of the pit. This so astonished him that he came running all the way back to the house to tell me.

We both went to take a look. In the meanwhile Mwangi, Gushu and Kimani were already in the hut, asking us to pass the torch to them. The wives began to emerge from their *rondavels* to see what all the excitement was about. Several men we had never set eyes on before, but who must have been visiting Mwangi, also came over. From the river bank more Africans appeared.

Mwangi emerged into the sunlight and held up his hand. He had an idea. He cackled at his wives, who all turned round and cackled at the youngest, the maid-of-all-work. They spoke in Kikuyu so we did not know what it was about until we saw the little creature return staggering under the weight of a large stone. As none of the others showed the least sign of going to her help, Billy relieved her of the stone.

He threw it down outside the little house. Mwangi picked it up, and, accompanied by Gushu, the wives, the friends and well-wishers, went inside again. Billy and I waited in the cold, bracing, morning air.

We heard the rock drop fifteen feet.

Out rushed the wives squealing, out came the friends; out tumbled Gushu; out staggered Mwangi. Wildly the two men glanced about them, got their bearings and made off for the river. The wives rolled with laughter on the ground, friends and well-wishers hugged each other, tears streaming out of their eyes. This kind of situation to the African was irresistibly funny.

Word got round to our Neighbour-to-the-West and the son came over after breakfast with his gun. The only way to kill the mamba in the pit was to shoot it, he said.

The three of us went down to the little house. I crouched out of the way, holding the torch as best I could so that the beam followed the snake round and round the floor of the pit. Standing astride the box our neighbour and Billy took pot-shots. But the angles were all wrong. There was much noise and smoke, my hand became numb on the torch, but the mamba remained unharmed.

"Burn it," our neighbour said.

We collected newspapers, crammed them down into the pit, poured paraffin and then went outside. Billy lighted a single sheet and watched it floating lazily down. The next instant there came a woomph! Thick white smoke burst out of the little house and Billy emerged choking, coughing and spluttering, with his face blackened and his eyebrows singed.

The snake was dead at last, but there was so much smoke now in the little house that to use it was out of the question. However, as it was the weekend, we packed a suitcase, collected Ralph and his impedimenta and set off to spend a couple of days at the Lake Hotel on the shores of Naivasha Lake.

7

THE rains were late that year, and because the previous rains had been poor, drought soon began to hit the colony. Vegetation withered away completely. Fissures opened in the earth. The pastoral tribes wandered despairingly with their emaciated cattle in search of grass. Lakes dwindled: several dried up altogether. Those rivers which survived the drought became little more than strings of stranded pools much fought over by thirsty animals trekking to them from great distances.

But the sunsets and the dawns at this time of year were splendid to see. The colours in the sky were vivid, primeval, reds like fresh-flowing blood, metallic yellows, vivid tangerines and a green as translucent as emeralds. Mount Kenya in its strawberry bonnet of ice and its crystal glaciers was a pale thing in comparison.

We played badminton in the evening until it was too dark to distinguish the shuttlecocks from the big white moths that came out of the veldt. We ate our dinner on the bald, iron-hard strip of earth outside the verandah which we hopefully referred to as the lawn. We kept a pressure-lamp burning in the dining-room (or lounge or what you will, there being only this other room apart from the one in which we slept). Like a lighthouse, the beams of this lamp glowed out over the veldt, seen, we were informed, even by our Neighbours-to-the-West when they sat out on their verandah. Moths streamed into the beams and bumped themselves against the wire mesh guards over the windows. Next morning their bodies lay in deep drifts over the window-sills.

There was always a sense of release, a freeing of the spirit that came to us when we sat outside at night. Stars were all about us, whether we craned our necks to stare up into the zenith, or just looked straight ahead at them twinkling from a little above ground level. We tried to count meteors, but gave up for they were too numerous.

Then there were the other stars, the eyes which would suddenly materialise in the blackness of the veldt verge, glow like living embers and disappear. We became expert at type identification, being able to distinguish in no time at all between the eyes of dik-dik, hare, bush-buck, nightjars and such like.

The eyes always excited Mbwa, the dog, who barked and chased after them. But there were certain other eyes, larger eyes, set farther apart and raised higher from the ground, staring out of the night. These caused hysterics. Her bark would turn into a scream as, flanks heaving, she would crouch between our chairs for protection. For these eyes we kept stones. Billy and I became adept at throwing stones and regularly scored direct hits. Next day we would find the pug-marks of a leopard in the dust.

The Lady Northy accepted Ralph. With heavy hearts we left him in the care of the nurses and returned to Shenzi Ville feeling too depressed to eat or even to talk. That was the night we went early to bed, took no notice when leopards drank out of the zinc bath, didn't look for snakes in the bed-clothes, and ignored the hyenas gibbering round the garbage-can.

I found myself a job on the editorial staff of the *East African Standard*. For some months previously this paper had been publishing articles of mine which I had written originally in an effort to collect enough money to buy Billy a Christmas present. I had never worked on a newspaper before, my experience up to then being limited to editing a women's journal for the Services during the war, and as a Press liaison officer in the Public Relations Directorate, New Delhi. Later in London I was employed by a firm of publishers.

When I was offered a salary of £25 a month to edit eleven pages of the paper's big weekend issue which came out on Fridays I readily accepted, for as I pointed out to them, I knew nothing about editing a newspaper. I commenced work immediately.

In the meanwhile, Shenzi Ville began to lower our morale. Billy hated lighting the lamps. Lamps should be lit, he declared, with the pressing down of a switch. I didn't like the way snakes made free with our abode.

Our only consolation then was Mbwa, the dog. She belonged to Mwangi. Mwangi never fed her, but she kept herself sleek and plump by her own efforts in the hunt.

The Africans must have held her prowess in the field in high esteem, for she had only to prick up her ears, flatten her little body, and they would be instantly on the alert. Off Mbwa would dart into the veldt, swift, light, sure. When she had killed, be it bird or hare or buck, out after her the Africans would rush, Mwangi and his male visitors caterwauling, hooting, throwing sticks and stones at her. Sometimes she got away with her lawful prey. Other times, they would run her to earth and steal her catch from her.

Though I saw no other dog as long as I lived at Shenzi Ville, Mbwa managed to get herself pregnant. Her husband must have been one of the veldt jackals. We awaited the birth with much interest.

Billy and I went off on a safari into the Marsabit area and the Lorian swamp, curious to see this part of Kenya, situated in the eastern half of the Northern Frontier District, which Martin Johnson had made famous. Marsabit, an extinct volcano rising 5,000 feet above the arid plains which surround it for hundreds of miles each way, causes passing clouds to loose their moisture upon it. The result is that the vegetation on its slopes is rich, green and blossoming, and breaks upon the vision of the heat-weary, dust-choked traveller with the fantasy of a fairy tale. When we saw Marsabit the forests were moth-eaten with the drought, and the streams had shrunk, but for all that we were greatly impressed. What must it look like in the rains ?

But it was a bad drought and everywhere we could discern marks of tragedy and devastation. We passed bone-thin elephants, their skin hanging on their skeletons like empty sacks. Giraffe and zebra, usually so plump and sleek, were emaciated, their coats no longer stretched over filled bellies, no longer glossy. They moved as if movement itself was too much of an effort.

But it was in the Lorian swamp that the full story of the drought became apparent. The swamp is about nine miles long, is fed by the River Uaso Nyiro, is three hundred and forty-five miles away from Nairobi and has, since the days of Martin Johnson, been famous for its big game and bird life.

But the Uaso Nyiro, rising in the snows of Mount Kenya, had been dry the past two months. An area affecting hundreds of square miles was all but waterless in consequence. Wells were drying up, and the Sabenna well in the heart of the swamp was about the only available source of water for man and beast.

Tribes drove their cattle and their goats over the deserts towards this precious place. Animals that still had enough strength to move a leg made weary pilgrimages to it.

We drove around the area. The sight which met our eyes was pitiful. Vegetation had withered to brittle stalks which rustled about us, rasping against the mudguards, as we dodged between the bodies of dead and dying animals. The smell of putrefying flesh was everywhere. Crevasses in the river-bed were choked with the bodies of game that had travelled great distances in search of water only to find none when they got there. We saw two elephants cemented together in hardened mud and not far off another so weak that all it could do as it lay on its side was to flap the edges of an ear. Camels lay on their sides, half dead, dead and dying. We saw a camel drop as it stood. It had been standing still for a long time, dying on its feet.

We heard stories of elephants that hung around the deep wells in the Lorian, waiting till the natives fetched up water, to frighten them off and help themselves. Sometimes, when a man looked up and saw an elephant waiting for him to come out of the well, he would just stay on inside. These wells are not wells as we know them. They are nothing more than large deep pits cut into the ground. Once we were told that an elephant, waiting in vain for the man to come up again with his giraffe-hide buckets of water, lost its temper and trampled in so much of the brim of the well that the man was almost buried alive.

We returned to Shenzi Ville to find a tent pitched on the river-banks. I asked Gushu whose tent it was and he said that a *Bwana* and a *Memsaab* had come to live there. By his tone and his look it was obvious that the couple were thoroughly unwelcome.

On my return from work the next day I went over to call on the campers and offer them the hospitality of my house — such as it was. Mbwa tagged along too as she invariably did whenever we went walking anywhere.

As I approached the sound of a symphony came rolling incongruously out to me over the balding veldt. When I was within hailing distance of the tent a flap lifted, and out stepped a gentleman in full evening clothes and a lady in an evening gown.

"Don't look so surprised," she said, introducing herself. The name was Pidgeon. "We heard all about you from mutual friends and were meaning to call, but you've been away over the weekend. If I may, I'd like to call over tomorrow."

The Pidgeons were going to a reception at Government House that evening. I learned later that they had bought a farm upcountry and were waiting to take possession. Into the safari wagon they climbed and bumped away over the trackless veldt towards our road.

We had never heard of jiggers. We had no idea they existed until our feet turned sore and walking became distressful. Small swellings appeared in the more tender parts of our feet, in the skin between the toes, under the arches, along the cuticles. The swellings were the size of a grain of barley and very painful to the touch.

Gushu found us ruefully contemplating our feet on the strip of verandah when he brought us our early morning tea. He placed the tray on the table and took our feet one by one in his hands, examined them and pronounced "jeegars!"

Jiggers, he said, were minute flies that were to be found in the soil, particularly the kind of virgin soil we had about us. These flies had laid their eggs under the skin of our feet. The barley grains were the sacks containing the jiggers' eggs and had to be removed immediately before they hatched out.

He fetched a needle which Billy sterilised over the flame of his cigarette-lighter. Then, squatting down in front of us, Gushu very gently opened up the skin above each barley grain and pulled the flaps apart to reveal a pinky-white sac, which, taking infinite pains not to break, he lifted out and placed on a piece of paper. A hollow in the flesh remained as a souvenir of the jigger's maternal activities.

In all he collected fourteen barley grains. He was scandalised. The time had come to deliver a lecture on the evils of going about in sandals with the vulnerable skin of our feet positively inviting jiggers to lay their eggs in it.

"Jeegar very bad. You must ask doctor to give you medicine to make jeegar not come on your feets."

Skirting our cleared patch and making off towards the squatters' quarters we saw an African come limping, the morning sun shining brilliantly on his rags, his greasy skin and the huge scars which covered his chest and face. He was Mwangi's brother and the scars had been made by a leopard in a hand-to-hand fight.

"See that man coming?" Gushu said, pointing. "That Mwangi's brother, Njeroga. See how he walk. Side to side to side. You know why he cannot walk properly? He have too much jeegar. Jeegar eat up his feet. He is a dirty savage."

Upon the veldt the wind blew with unrestrained vigour. It began its life round about ten o'clock with no more than a playful lifting of the wattle leaves, a coy rustling in the dry grass. By eleven, the leaves in the the passion-fruit creeper rubbed fretfully against each other, and tiny eddies of loose earth had begun to spiral upwards a foot or two. The wind had a long way to come. It blew in from the Indian Ocean hundreds of miles away, passing over the sun-riven coastal belts, forced up into cooler, higher air by the rising land, three thousand feet, four, five, six. As it rose it gathered speed. Over the lava deserts it sped, over the barren sand deserts, making for the Highlands with concentrated fury.

The Highlands straddle the equator and the noonday sun shines from directly overhead, consuming all shadows. It is never hot because of the high altitudes, but the dryness is dehydrating. From noon to two o'clock the sun lets loose a deluge of light so powerful that colours bleach white under it and everything seems to become incandescent. It is a time when the wind is at its liveliest.

Great gusts swoop over the land, whipping up the dust. Thermal currents draw up the heated air to form dust-devils. These dust-devils are great whirling columns of uprushing air, raising tons of soil hundreds of feet into the sky. They rush over the veldt like a pack of genii and everything they pass over gets sucked up into their flying towers.

Whenever I saw a dust-devil approach I would dash into the house and bang the door shut. To be caught in one was to be turned into a pillar of dust, choked, temporarily blinded. I have seen a black man overtaken by one and emerge red from head to foot.

One afternoon a dust-devil got caught up with the lean-to kitchen. I heard the familiar rush and roar, then a shattering sound. By the time I had rushed to the window and the atmosphere had cleared sufficiently to see, the galvanised iron sheets which comprised the kitchen were bowling giddily over the veldt. However, that evening Mwangi, Gushu, Kimani and all the *rafikis* set out on a search for the galvanised sheeting, the braziers and pots and pans. By nightfall all was as it had been before.

At that time there was another wind blowing through Kenya, an uglier wind and more deadly. . . .

Gushu openly showed his dislike of the Pidgeons. When questioned he couldn't say why he did not like them. Mwangi, all his wives and *rafikis* made it clear that they too shared this antipathy.

Naturally the Pidgeons were unwelcome. It was not till later that we learned they had innocently set up camp in the very spot where Mwangi and his *rafikis* held their nocturnal meetings and their *pombe* parties. Everywhere in Kenya at this period Kikuyus were collecting in groups, holding meetings, spreading the word of Mau Mau among the tribe. They were planning a reign of terror and bloodshed. Kikuyus were taking oaths to kill Europeans. The oaths were made voluntarily or by coercion. Those who would not take the oath were summarily put to death and interred in shallow graves. These graves and their contents were not discovered till terrorism had broken out in the Colony, and then it was seen from severed wrists and ankles, from split skulls, from rudely chopped limbs, that the victims had not been slain quickly but had been subjected to forms of torture as well. And the eyes that had beheld such scenes, the Kikuyu servants and clerks and office boys, kept their secrets, revealing nothing to the Europeans who employed them.

One evening our Neighbours-to-the-West called on us. They had brought along with them the head of the house of our Neighbours-to-the-South. It seemed that their properties had been raided the previous night, chickens had been stolen, goats and even a cow. How the thieves had got away with them no one knew. The stolen stock had not offered up a squeak of protest. True there had been many footprints in the dust of the *shamba* grounds, but the wily thieves had taken their booty over the veldt where no tracks could be traced. One theory was that the chickens, goats and cow had been loaded into a lorry and driven away. Police had been called. By the time investigations had begun it was late afternoon and dust-devils had obliterated what clues there were.

"We'll never catch the rascals now," said our neighbours.

They had planned a counter-raid on all squatter families in the district. The raid was to be secret. Billy was invited to join the raiders. They planned to meet about midnight and then to search every squatter colony for traces of freshly killed meat, for new hides, for *pombe*, and indeed for anything which might lead to the capture of the thieves.

Billy did not like the idea, but on the other hand to back out when the neighbours so clearly expected him to help them was not possible either. Neither he nor I believed that Mwangi, Gushu, Kimani and the guileless-looking *rafikis* could have had a hand in the stealing of our neighbours' livestock. We said so.

"The African is a crafty creature," we were told. "Don't you be taken in by his childish ways. Underneath he is cunning and unpredictable. You may think he is loyal, but he is treacherous. Don't you trust your servants. We hear that strange gatherings take place on the river-bank out there."

At midnight Billy slipped out of the house. It was not a dark night, for though there was no moon the stars were luminous enough. From the window I could see him quite clearly as he joined the silent, muffled figures on the road. I went to another window from where I could see the *rondavels* behind Shenzi Ville.

All was peaceful and quiet there. No voice was raised in song, no hand beat a drum. We had become accustomed by now to the sound of drums beating and voices crooning well into the small hours. In the starlight, those toadstool *rondavels* looked so innocent that I knew without a shadow of doubt warning of the raid had been passed to them.

Billy returned at about four o'clock, bone-weary, cold and dusty. The raid had been a complete fiasco. Every Kikuyu colony they visited was a model of rectitude. Some of the men had even grown indignant on the Europeans' behalf, offering to join them in the search for wrongdoers.

"They had the laugh on us all right," Billy said. "The others are furious, but what can they do?"

Gushu was in high spirits next day. He crooned songs as he worked. Twice he forgot himself sufficiently to call me Mama to my face. (Usually this appellation was reserved for use behind my back.) When he brought me my elevenses, it being Saturday and I not at work, he said. "My *bwana* is good. But other *bwana* come and make for my *bwana* to be bad."

Mornings were a bad time with Gushu. He would arrive with bloodshot eyes and marks of strain on his ugly giraffe face. But this morning he looked fresh and perky, no doubt having benefited from a good night's sleep.

He giggled. "When Roosians come to Kenya they send settlers away. Old settlers bad. They say African is dirty savage."

"What do you know about Russians?"

That was the first occasion Gushu mentioned Russians. I must have thought it sufficiently significant for I have entered it in my diary. The date is 23 Feb. 1948.

"Roosians is good friends for African. He say we are his brother. He say never mind the black skin. African has same colour blood and same colour bones as him. So African is his friend, his comrade, his brother. When Roosian come there will be no rich European with big *shamba* and many cows and much money. Roosians will take away from the European and give to the poor African. I like the Roosian."

In the diary is noted:

"Pointed out to G. fallacy of his argument. Enlightened him on Russian methods, etc. Said that Europeans had brought wealth and prosperity to Kenya. Europeans work hard. I don't think he believes me."

When I repeated this conversation to Billy and to my fellow editors in the office, they saw nothing ominous in it. But I wondered at the time how Gushu had got such ideas into his head.

Mbwa disappeared for two days. When she returned she was sleek again and her teats heavy with milk. We searched the grounds for her litter. I had a box prepared for the pups, but she had hidden them far out upon the veldt and kept their hiding-place a secret not to be shared even with us.

In our search, however, we did find half-buried *debis* of fomenting *pombe*. When Gushu and Mwangi were shown these *debis* they raised their hands in holy indignation, demanding of each other who could be so evil as to make their own alcoholic drinks. Never had those two innocents heard of such outrageous goings-on. We felt we should empty the *debis*, for the acrid smell was enough to turn anyone's stomach. Gushu and Mwangi agreed that it was an excellent thing to do. If we wished they would do the emptying themselves. All the wives and *rafikis* came round. Everyone protested loudly in righteous anger. Gushu grabbed one *debi* and tipped a little of its contents on the ground.

We left them to it. I knew they would not empty those *debis*, but as Billy and I saw it, the African was as much entitled to his sundowner as we were. We did not know, in our ignorance, the violence and hysteria, the blood lust, that alcohol can excite in the brain of primitive man.

One Saturday afternoon, when we were driving up the Thika road towards the Blue Post Inn which stands overlooking the Chania Falls, we noticed a thick white thunderhead of smoke rolling ominously over the veldt. A little further on flocks of terrified ostriches galloped across the road and made off in an easterly direction. The wind roared over the veldt and before it drove the thunderhead of smoke, much bigger now, rising thickly into the sky, travelling at great speed. We drew up on the grass verge to watch.

Over the crest of a wave of rising ground flowed the smoke and we caught sight of flames licking avidly under it. The rate at which that veldt fire moved was frightening to see. Forward, outward it spread, a tidal wave that nothing could stop.

"It's making in the direction of Shenzi Ville," Billy said. "With that wind behind it and at the pace it's going, I don't give it fifteen minutes to reach our place."

He swung the Cream Bun round and broke our hitherto modest speed records on the way back. Over the tarmacadam, turning sharply right, then over the bad dust track we sped, pausing only to let through a stampede of wild life, hare, deer, mongooses, ostrich again, bush buck, wart hogs, leopards, all united in a common terror, fleeing before the smoke and the flames.

We reached home, jumped out of the Cream Bun and saw to our amazement that already a wide band of blackened veldt surrounded Shenzi Ville and the squatters' *rondavels*. There were dozens of Africans on the property, all waving branches plucked from the young wattle that grew there.

"They've burned a fire-break," Billy said. "How the devil they did it, with the wind in the wrong quarter I don't know."

Mwangi hurried over, grave, responsible. He fussed and cackled. He ordered us not to fear. We were saved. The house was saved. The vehicle was saved. He, Mwangi, had saved us from the fire. A black and jubilant savage, clad in little more than his fez, waved a wattle branch gleefully at us from behind the burnt-out skeleton of some thorn bushes.

"You no frighten *Bwana, Memsaab*," Gushu yelled. With a flourish he belaboured a strip of grass that had long since ceased to burn, showing what a genius he was at quenching fires.

Where was Mbwa? We searched the house. We searched the grounds within the blackened ring of burnt-out grass. The fire was dashing fiercely towards us with the roar of an express train. The blue sky was gone, obliterated by smoke. We saw Mbwa breaking through the veldt verge beyond the ring of burnt-out grass. She was carrying a pup in her mouth.

She whimpered with pain as she trod the hot ashes. Her fur was singed. Billy ran to her, picked her up, puppy and all, and brought her back to the clearing. When he set her on her feet she trotted off to the lean-to garage and put down the puppy, pushing it under a piece of sacking. There were two others there already, eyes not yet opened.

I hurried indoors to fetch a bowl of milk, but Mbwa had gone back to the veldt, her mission not yet over. By now the fire was very near and coming nearer every moment. The heat of it licked about us. It was as if an oven heated to about 450 degrees was suddenly flung wide. In the high, cold veldt, where at this hour we would normally be slipping into warm coats, we found ourselves streaming with sweat.

Billy tried to stop the dog, but she struggled furiously out of his grasp and was away, making straight for the oncoming wave of flame. Helplessly we stood and watched. The sky was stained tea-colour with smoke. The roar of the fire was loud in our ears. Just ahead of the flames hovered hundreds of birds of prey, kites, hawks, eagles, storks. They hovered, wings beating, heads bent, eyes intent on the creatures frantically trying to escape from the onrushing wave. It was a field day for those birds. Rabbits, young deer and snakes were caught up in relentless talons and carried away.

The wave flooded about us, broke away

at the area which had already been burned, closed round the property, raising the temperature unbearably, then fled on, leaving us unharmed.

Night came. All that was left of the fire was a red glow to the south. It had travelled many miles by then. We noticed, however, that fire still burned redly where our Neighbours-to-the-West lived. Long after the rest of the wave had vanished southwards and our part of the veldt lay still and burned out, those fires went on burning.

At about nine o'clock Billy and I decided to go and have a look. We got into the Cream Bun and drove over. The flames we could see from our place were made by a copse of eucalyptus trees burning steadily. We had been told that these forty-foot high trees had been planted when our neighbours first came out here many years ago. There would be nothing left of them now. Neither, we saw, would there be very much left of the house, the go-downs, the cattle sheds, the goat sheds, the chicken coops, the servants' quarters. Our Neighbours-to-the-West, who had gone for a day's outing in Nairobi, were going to have a shock when they returned.

Where were their servants, and why had they done nothing to save their employer's property? We asked ourselves that question standing in the deserted *shamba*, staring about us and seeing only desolation in the light of the flaming eucalyptus trees.

The next morning we awoke to a veldt in mourning. It was as if a sable cloak had been spread over the earth and in contrast the vivid sky and the coloured snows of Mount Kenya were all the more striking.

The only living creature within sight was our friend the ant bear, pallid and grotesque, picking his way over the ashes. We found Mbwa's body. It lay beside her last puppy.

When Gushu came we wanted to know why none of our neighbours' servants had done anything to save their employers' property. The eucalyptus trees still smoked and we could just see the skeleton of walls from where we stood.

"I don't know," Gushu said, drawing a long face and shaking his head. "Fire very bad. Now they must go live another place. *Shauri ya Mungu.*" It is the will of God.

8

OUR lives followed a new routine. We were on our way to our respective offices by eight in the morning. We met and lunched together at an hotel. In the evenings, before returning to Shenzi Ville, we spent an hour with Ralph, and this meant that by the time we were home again it was the hour for lighting up the oil-lamps and cooking the evening meal.

People could talk of nothing then but the absent rains. They looked up into the cold pale skies, cloudless and brazen, searching for the first signs of the promised monsoon. Any day now, we said. Prophecies were made. The fifteenth of March. That was the day the rains should break. But the fifteenth came and went with not so much as a tatter of cloud to soften the unrelenting sky. Reports of thirst-mad animals migrating down the river-beds towards the coast, wreaking havoc as they went, appeared daily in the *Standard*. In my section of the paper I found myself including more and more harrowing stories of human and animal sufferings, all connected with the failure of last season's rains and the delay in the present ones. Farmers up-country began talking of famine.

Kenya knew very well what famine could mean. There had been long famines before when Africans set out from their Reserves in long hunger marches to the capital, many dying on the way. During the famine of 1916, the hyenas, a missionary once told me, were so gorged with the flesh of dead bodies that when she and twenty-eight Kikuyu women were making a safari from the mission in Tumutumu to Fort Hall to fetch back a few sacks of grain, hyenas attacked them one night as they slept under canvas, seeking to devour the living as an alternative to the dead. Famines hit the African hardest, for he never stored his grain or looked beyond his day's needs. To put away for a rainy day, or as in Kenya's case, a non-rainy season, was alien to his nature.

March slipped away and yet no rain fell. Billy began to look round for another place for us to live. We were both beginning to lose heart. Our African venture was not turning out at all well. To make matters worse I was running into rough weather in the office.

As the only woman on the editorial staff, I had been given a room to myself. But in the room was a wireless set. Twice a day someone came in and took down the B.B.C. news bulletins. While this went on it was impossible to concentrate.

My window overlooked a closed-in yard. In consequence so little of the bright African day reached inside the room that I worked in a perpetual grey gloom. Apart from the wireless set there was also a large wooden contraption, eight feet long by two feet wide and about four feet high. A local *fundi* had put it together and it held the entire records of the *Standard*, and its boneyard. Reporters, subs, secretaries were constantly pulling out its shelves, constantly consulting its contents.

Above me on the next floor was the photographic and block-making department. When machinery wasn't humming, the block-makers could be heard hammering industriously. In the courtyard below there was a constant coming and going of iron-wheeled handcarts bringing packages to the packing and distributing department on the floor beneath me. African office boys hung out in the courtyard, sitting on up-turned boxes, chattering and laughing.

But all this I took in my stride.

Even the weekly row with the sports editor, who laid claim to two columns of my section, lost its terrors. It was never my fault, and he knew it, when I had to deprive him of some of his space in order to give more prominence to the activities of the Legislative Council. The sports columns in my section were considered fair game if anything more interesting cropped up.

By and by even the extraordinary happenings down at the works did not seem so lunatic after all. At that time the linotype operators were mostly men who could neither speak nor read English. My favourite tormentors, who were responsible for carrying out my lay-out, setting up the formats, and generally getting the pages ready for press, were not mentally deficient, but gave a good imitation of being so. I don't think they even glanced at the carefully-thought-out lay-out pages I sent down to them, nor bothered to read my very explicit instructions.

Proof sheets when they came up to me were never without their surprises. An article on the filming of *King Solomon's Mines* complete with photographs of the stars would appear under a headline on the prevalence of tapeworm among Africans.

"Why? Why? In the name of goodness why?" I would plead of the bored operator. After three minutes of blank staring, he would put one finger under his hair and scratch up the dandruff on his scalp. "Both haf three column," would be the brilliant explanation.

It was the same with photographs and captions. So long as a caption fitted under a block, it did not matter whether the two were related or not. Woodcuts taxed the ingenuity of the operators still further. They never seemed to know which way up they should go into the formes. All the little lines made them cross-eyed. In deep bewilderment they would turn the blocks round and round. Whenever woodcuts were to appear in my pages I had to be on the alert. Once I got down to the works in time to hold up the printing of an issue which showed a beautifully executed wood-cut of the Chania Falls turned the wrong way up so that the Falls gushed upwards.

All these things I was able to take in my stride. Even the extra reporting work, the interviews I was sent out to do and the social events I was expected to write up. Celebrities were constantly coming to Kenya. It was a privilege to meet and talk to such people, even though it often meant forgoing my evening session with Ralph and returning home at all hours of the night.

"I would refuse if I were you," the subs and the reporters said. "You were engaged to edit the Friday magazine section. Not to do all this other work. I'd refuse."

"You aren't being paid extra for it, are you?"

"Of course you know what's behind all this," they said. "Kidondo wants to get rid of you. He hates women. With every woman we've had on the staff he has done everything in his power to make life intolerable for her. He's up to his routine tricks."

Kidondo is a Swahili word which means "boil, ulcer or sore place". It was the nickname the African workers had bestowed upon the little fat man who sat in the room next to mine. His room had a carpet and was luxuriously furnished. His fine big desk was drawn up immediately on the other side of mine. Had there not been the wall we could have touched elbows. Into this wall was let a hatch. But the hatch had been boarded up. I did not at first notice that a small round peep-hole had been bored into it.

Kidondo peeped because he was the peeping kind. He also eavesdropped. Reporters or subs opening his door without warning often caught him straining over on his side, ear clamped to the peep-hole, listening avidly to what I was saying on the phone or to a visitor.

One day while I was on the phone to someone, I noticed the hole in the hatch for the first time and absent-mindedly stuck my pencil into it. There followed a squeak and a curse. For days after Kidondo went about with a shield over his eye. Immediately after I found myself on the mat, brought before the editor-in-chief, Mr. Kinnear, on the charge of not writing enough for the paper.

I explained in vain that I was doing a

considerable amount of writing — reports, social functions, interviews and so on. But Kidondo was there, making sure that I did not get off too lightly.

"You were engaged to write humorous articles — like the ones you wrote for us before you came here," he said in his small fat voice.

"It's all I can do to keep up with my present assignments," I said.

I was told to go away and provide more original copy. I gave the matter some considerable thought. Why not write up the stories of Kenya's women pioneers? I had already met and made friends with some of these courageous, gallant women, and the stories they had to tell of their early pioneering days were more thrilling than any American Western.

In the meanwhile Billy heard from a friend of a friend that there was a house available about ten miles or so from Nairobi along the Ngong road. He showed me a snapshot of the house and I fell in love with the place straight away. It was like an English cottage, half smothered with roses. The name was appropriately chosen. It was called Rose Cottage.

Billy made arrangements for us to go and see it. The owner was leaving on a prolonged visit to Britain and would be away for a year, perhaps even two or three. "If we like the place," Billy said, for once looking on the optimistic side, "we could spend the rest of our tour there and say to blazes with this long-promised Government accommodation."

Kidondo began to set up people against me. He went up to the photographic department and had a word with the gentleman who ran it. When next I went up there with a sheaf of photographs, this gentleman warned me of Kidondo's campaign. "He's going right through the establishment," I was informed. "He's even been speaking to the Goans in the works, the proof readers, and the chaps down in the shop."

I found myself being sent out on assignments to the African Reserves. But this the management came to know about and stopped in a very short time. I waited to see what the fat man would do next.

I didn't wait long. The previous Friday I had published among other wedding photographs one of a young lieutenant and his bride. The bridegroom carried a sword.

The sword was the property of a bustling little cock-sparrow of a major, a buddy of Kidondo's. The major had read the report of the wedding which I had written, and noted that I did not mention the fact that the sword was really the major's and was only *lent* to the groom for the occasion.

On the Saturday the major marched in to Kidondo. I couldn't help hearing much fierce whispering going on in the next room. A few minutes later in burst the major, moustache abristle, thumping my table with his fist and demanding to know why I had omitted such an important piece of information. I held my ground. I told him I did not think the sword was at all important to the wedding report. He grew red in the face, thumped and blustered, and then took himself off to complain about me to the editor.

That was the last I heard of the incident. Mr. Kinnear never brought it up.

But I had had enough. My pen was full. I unscrewed the cap, placed the nib against the peep-hole and squirted the entire contents into Kidondo's earhole. From that time my days at the *Standard* were numbered.

Mr. Kinnear liked my idea of writing up Kenya's pioneer women. He gave me the names of suitable pioneers and promised to put me in touch with more. My first pioneer was Agnes Shaw of Sotik.

Every week I met more and more of these fine women. Their stories were epics of courage, endurance and that doggedness of spirit which refuses to admit defeat. Into a lifetime each had packed adventures, thrills, breathtaking experiences which were all but incredible. For the first time since I began work at the *Standard* I found myself liking my job.

Billy in the meanwhile had fixed up for us to pay a call on the owner of Rose Cottage. The next evening after work we were to go out and see the place. The rent was remarkably low and Rose Cottage from the photographs we had seen looked a very different proposition from Shenzi Ville. Here was a real dwelling-place, not the nucleus of one.

"Of course," said Billy, "it's a bit off the beaten track and on the edge of the Game Reserve."

9

ON the 2nd of April, after office hours, we went to look at Rose Cottage. The directions were simple. The house stood fourteen to fifteen miles from Nairobi Post Office and all we had to do was to follow the road.

There was no time for anything but the briefest visit to Ralph. On a good road the Cream Bun would have made short work of the distance. But the corrugations on that particular stretch being fiercer, the pot-holes larger than any we had as yet encountered, speed was out of the question. The bone structure of our respective bodies received a brisk shaking up. Nature had planted tough teeth in our heads or we should have spat out mouthfuls after the first five miles.

On we rattled in grand style. Decorous houses standing serenely in their own spacious gardens gave way to open veldt and light forest. Down went the sun behind the Ngong Hills, up radiated rays like the spokes of a wheel, bright orange against an apple-green sky. We were now in arid country, rough, dried-out with withered grass on either side of the road tall enough to hide a herd of buffalo.

"Imagine having to make this journey twice a day," we said to each other. Colour drained swiftly out of the sky, and the air became subtly tinted with the greys of a pigeon's wing, mysterious, deceptive, yet not dark enough to warrant switching on the headlamps. We were ready to call it a day and return when we saw the road rise and pass over the brow of a hill.

"We'll go up there and have just one last look round," Billy said.

As we drew near the hill we saw a group of figures outlined against the pigeon-wing sky. We took them to be a road gang returning from work, or perhaps a hunting party of Africans; it was difficult to tell in that uncertain light. They might know where we would find Rose Cottage.

A pot-hole six feet in diameter and a foot deep pitted the road. By the time we had skirted it safely we lifted our eyes to see about us a pride of lions. These were what we had mistaken for Africans. The engine stalled. Quickly we rolled up the windows and waited.

The lions were not particularly surprised by our presence. Some rose in a leisurely manner from the sun-warmed dust and strolled over. One climbed on the bonnet and regarded us sharply for a few seconds. One or two sniffed round the mudguards and a three-quarter-grown cub bent its head in such a way that we felt he was going to try his teeth on the front near-side tyre. The head of the family did no more than rise on his haunches and fix his large clear eyes, strangely luminous in that owl-light, upon the vehicle. The wind-screen became misty with lion's breath.

Billy sounded a fanfare on his horn and started up the engine. We shot off at a spanking pace, tumbled the lioness off the bonnet, stopped the venturesome cub from biting the tyre and generally scattered the scandalised pride to left and right.

Over that hill and we were coasting down a long slope that dipped some six or seven hundred feet towards a green valley. Even in that drought-ridden climate the valley was green and we could see and smell the freshness of it as we drove down the road.

Rose Cottage stood in the valley, its windows glowing with light — electric light we could see as we approached. The beat of a generating plant throbbed through the velvety night.

The drive was gravelled and sloped down to the front verandah. The whole house stood on concrete piers and was raised some ten feet or so above the ground. The gap between floor and ground was effectively screened by oleander and hibiscus bushes, all green and fresh-looking in the light of the headlamps. The car lights also illuminated the long flight of steps to the verandah, the low balustrade which surrounded it and the roses, such a profusion of roses, entwining pillars and bowers and archways. We alighted and were enchanted by the fragrance of roses.

The owner was middle-aged, very much the Colonel ex-Poona type, which indeed he was. His wife had left him to go and live in Bermuda with a man who had made his fortune in East African diamonds.

We were given a drink and then shown round the house. There were three large bedrooms, each about twenty-four feet by sixteen feet. The colonel was accustomed to large rooms. The drawing-room and dining-room were also built on a large scale. The bathroom, white-tiled, with an enamel bath and a porcelain wash-basin, seemed beautiful in our eyes after having put up with the zinc coffin and the chipped chamber service of Shenzi Ville.

"No outside lavatory, you will notice," he said.

The kitchen was banished beyond a barricade of bushes which were in too-dark shadow to identify. A covered way connected kitchen with main house and as far as we could make out this part of the establishment seemed to have been built of mud-and-wattle. The colonel suffered from ulcers in the stomach and couldn't stand the smell of food cooking.

"I live mostly at the Nairobi Club," he said, "but come out here for the weekends. I keep my cook and headboy here. They look after the place when I'm away."

The full moon rose. We went out on the verandah again. The bungalow stood in a trough of land which was slung, hammockwise, between the high sloping veldt down which we had come and a sharply rising forested area. It faced down the trough towards undulating open veldt which merged into the Game Reserve. The views of Kilimanjaro, Africa's snow-capped and highest mountain, 19,455 ft., were excellent, we were told, from not only the front verandah but from the drawing-room and other windows of the house as well. Connecting the verandah with the gravel drive was a picturesque wooden bridge, smothered in honeysuckle and roses. We admired the bridge and never thought to inquire whether its purpose was other than ornamental.

"As far as I am concerned you may move in tomorrow," he said generously.

We stayed on to dinner, having been pressed, for the colonel was delighted to hear that we ourselves had spent two years during the war in India and were familiar with places long beloved by him. The meal was excellent. His cook was a jewel, he said. We might keep him on if we wished, but the headboy wanted to leave. This arrangement suited us. In our establishment we could not have anyone but Gushu as the headboy.

We made arrangements to move in the following week-end, paid three months' rent in advance, and left with happy hearts.

At once the weather underwent a change. That same night, clouds, the merest tatters to be sure, began to drift over the full moon. By morning galleons were ploughing before a moisture-laden wind. On the day we moved into Rose Cottage the heavens opened and down bucketed the rain.

On Monday morning it was all Billy could do to push the Cream Bun out of the foot-deep mire which surrounded the house on to the upper reaches of the drive. The cook, Gushu, Kimani and one of the cook's *rafikis* who had come to help push, retired covered from head to foot in rich red mud. For the first time I realised that the bridge was not entirely for the purpose of holding up honeysuckle and climbing roses.

The pot-holes had filled with water. The corrugations were submerged. By the time we had come down the hill, left the open veldt and the forest behind us and were splashing down the road where it ran between houses and gardens, it was obvious that what had once been a highway was now the district's main drain. Vehicles cleft through the water in fine style, wearing a bow wave like a moustache on their fenders.

We had had high hopes of bringing Ralph home, but now this was out of the question. He was safer at the Lady Northy. To make matters worse our evening visits had to be cut short, for it was too risky trying to make the Rose Cottage road after dark.

For the same reason my after-office assignments developed into a nightmare.

"Look here," my fellow-workers on the *Standard* said to me, "pocket your pride and tell Kidondo it's sheer murder to send you out on evening jobs. After all the man must be human. He ought to understand."

Two of the reporters who lived in Nairobi itself offered to do my assignments for me. They would not be going out of their way, they said; besides, their wives would like to attend the more lively functions.

My salary, thanks to George Boyd, the chief sub-editor, who had pleaded on my behalf, had been raised from £25 a month to £40. Kidondo had tried to stop this rise coming through, but failed. It was difficult to see him taking a kindly view now of my request to be let off after-office assignments.

However, I tried. I told him of my circumstances, the bad road and the risk. He listened. He stared, blinking his pale eyes and disturbing the scallops of flesh which hung over his Adam's apple by swallowing two or three times in succession. The upshot of this interview was that I found myself being sent out on more after-office-hour assignments than ever.

"Chuck it," Billy said. "Tell them to go to hell."

But I would not. When I left the *Standard* it would be on my own terms . . . .

The rains were good. The parched earth lay under grateful floods. Within a week vegetation began to grow again, trees put out leaf-buds and the jacarandas down Delamere Avenue were vivid with spring-time's burgeoning.

We always carried in those days a powerful torch, jack-boots and a long stick in the Cream Bun. Billy also kept his rifle handy. These came in very useful when we had to get home after dark.

Some of my assignments called for

evening gown, some for cocktail dress. Whichever was needed I would take along with me and change into after work before going off on a job. Billy sometimes came with me, but when this was not possible he would stop off at the Club and call for me later.

On our journey back, I would change again, this time in the back of the Cream Bun. Into slacks, pullover and jackboots I'd get. When we reached that part of the road where the water had risen and sub-merged the crater-like holes I would get out and walk in front of the car, poking the ground with the stick, searching out the craters so that the vehicle could avoid them. Billy would follow after me in low gear, all windows rolled down and his loaded rifle, with the safety-catch off, on the seat beside him. The district had a bad name for lions.

Rose Cottage was soon marooned in the centre of a lake. The whole trough of the valley in which it stood gushed with springs that came to active life with the rains. The bridge was submerged and after three days of non-stop downpour, water began to lap over the verandah floorboards.

Billy had to park the Cream Bun half a mile or so away and six hundred feet above the valley. When we retired each night we asked ourselves whether the vehicle would be still there by morning.

"This place no good," Gushu kept saying. "You must take another house."

Crossing over from the house to that part of the drive which rose above the flood was not particularly precarious, for the bridge, though submerged, lay only four or five inches under water. A thick deposit of mud on the boards made the going slippery and sometimes, if the rain had fallen with unusual abundance, a fair current swept over it, but this was never strong enough to be a real danger.

Within an hour of the monsoon bursting, frogs came out around Rose Cottage in their hundreds. I had never seen so many frogs before. It was an invasion. They were everywhere, under beds, inside shoes, on chairs, among clothes. We waged a campaign against them and succeeded after a while in keeping all but the boldest out of the living-rooms and bedroom. Gushu had instructions to sweep away all frogs from the verandah before we came out of a morning to drink our early cup of tea.

The first sound which greeted us at daybreak would be Gushu sweeping frogs. He hated them bitterly and scolded as he wielded the broom. Sitting up in bed and watching him at it through the window I noticed that the frogs evinced a strong dislike for the cold muddy water and became adept at jumping anywhere, even on Gushu himself, rather than take the plunge. Those that did get thrown in were out again, making love for all they were worth, all over the verandah, before Gushu had so much as put his broom away.

Mildew spread like a skin desease over the damp walls. Surfaces of furniture, of shoes, became clammy to the touch. On washdays it was nearly impossible to dry clothes.

Then fuel ran out. The woodshed had been well stocked with dry logs. As we had fires only at night, these, even when used by us and the servants for cooking purposes, should have lasted us through the rains. Within a week the cook informed us that there were no logs left, that a relative of his had died and he must leave at once.

Would we give him a full month's pay in advance?

When he had gone we learned what had happened to all the logs. Cook was a generous man. He had many *rafikis* upon whom he bestowed, among other commodities which did not belong to him, logs from the woodshed. He was himself partial to a good roaring fire. While we were at the office all day, cook would take up residence in the drawing-room, disporting himself in the big leather arm-chair, while Kimani kept the fire blazing merrily. Cook also entertained in the drawing-room, his friends sitting with him drinking tea and sampling Billy's precious store of cigars.

Gushu gallantly offered to do the cooking. After three mornings of cold burnt toast, leathery porridge, rancid cream, raw bacon and greasy eggs, I took over.

Thanks to the owner's fastidiousness the kitchen stood a good twenty-five yards from the house and the connecting covered-way was now eight to nine inches under water. I began to fear for the safety of the kitchen itself. Unlike the main house it did not stand on piles but was built into a sharply rising bank. Water flowed unrestricted over the floor. The mud-and-wattle construction became so soaked that it was a wonder the whole thing did not disintegrate.

We asked Gushu about the servants' quarters. Were they dry? He said they were. "But this no good place. Too much animal in forest. You must get another house," he said.

After seven weeks of constant downpours the rains began to thin out. The intervals between one deluge and another gradually lengthened until sometimes, for several hours in the morning or afternoon, no rain fell at all. A wan and watery sun now began to show whitely in the flying wrack of clouds.

The lake about Rose Cottage subsided into a four-foot-deep cauldron of rich, bubbling mud. This was the signal for a succession of plagues to attack us.

First came the blackbeetle plague. Walls, furniture, clothes and curtains crawled with these slow-moving creatures. They fell into food, they crunched underfoot, they left minute feathery trails all over the place.

Next came flying-ants with their soft, squelchy bodies and gossamer wings that dropped off at a breath to thicken in deep drifts upon every surface — furniture, windows, and floor. These masochistic creatures, who were supposed to be at the height of their mating season, appeared to be bent on annihilation. They put themselves where they would be trodden upon; they clustered in door-jambs. The morning after the invasion, Gushu swept out basketfuls of dead bodies into the mud, where lizards and frogs eagerly disposed of them. We wondered how many of these flying-ants had remained alive to propagate their species.

Within ten days of the ants came the little hairless black caterpillars. These were about an inch long and were possessed of more enterprise than either the frogs or the ants, for they got inside pockets, under collars and into underclothing.

But as unexpectedly as they had come so they went, vanishing obediently as if at a given signal. Now it was the turn of the rats.

One night we went to bed without a sign of a rat anywhere in the vicinity of Rose Cottage. The next morning we awoke to see a rat sitting up on its hind legs on the dressing-table. The rats came in scores, not in hundreds of thousands as did the others. They were not as omnipresent either as the caterpillars, but they were nerve-rackingly audible. While the rat plague lasted we never got the sound of gnawing and scampering out of our ears.

We bought rat-traps and we laid down poison. The poisoned rats sought out the most difficult places to go and die in. Three dead bodies were found floating in the rainwater storage-tank. The water collected in this tank was supposed to last us till the next rains. We had to let the whole lot out.

Billy opened his brief-case in the office one morning and found a dead rat snugly rolled up inside some sketch plans. It looked bad, he told me, because with him were several Branch Heads who had come specially to see those plans.

For all this, Rose Cottage was not without its peculiar charm. After the rains the veldt turned an apple green, and to us as we sat on the verandah, gazing over the serene spaciousness, it looked like a billowing length of shot-silk. A profusion of wild flowers, some scarlet, some brilliant blue and gold and white, wove formless patterns into its waving expanse. Kilimanjaro constantly appeared, a vision that the sunrise and the sunset summoned up from the rims of space. The hill slopes under the forest were a riot of gaudy blossom.

I gathered these flowers whenever I had the time and brought them into the house. Some lasted for days, others would die within the hour. Blue and white delphinium and flame-coloured gladioli blew gaily in the wind. Orchids trailed from branches, and climbing up the trunks of larger trees was the orange thunbergia. Forget-me-nots, begonias pure white and fragile-seeming, the turquoise blue *parochetus major*, carpeted the forest's slopes with colour.

The butterflies came again. The veldt and the forest twinkled with the flutter of white or yellow wings, and sometimes, alas, the radiators of vehicles became plastered with dead bodies. Birds came frequently; from the honey-suckers and bee-eaters with whirring enamel-bright wings, to the sun-birds, the swallows, the thrushes, the bul-buls, and the pintailed widow-bird that trailed its foot-long tail before its mate's entranced gaze during the course of his wooing. Large birds came too: hawks, kites, vultures. By watching the flight of vultures across the sky we could predict the direction in which the lions would set out to kill that night, for those grisly birds had unfailing foreknowledge of death.

Guinea-fowl lived in flocks about the thickets that ran along the boundaries of the property. Regularly Gushu presented us with a succulent young one which he said he had brought down with a stone. I used to cook these either as a *fricassée* with a little red wine mixed with the gravy, or roasted and served with giblet sauce and red-currant jelly. In spite of Gushu's efforts at the hunt, these birds showed no trace of fear. They ran about the lawns and under the bushes with the familiarity of domestic chickens.

We liked the evenings best, when with ice-cool sundowners in our hands, our feet up on the low balustrade, we leaned back in our chairs and watched the drama of the veldt unfold before us. As the sun sank into the west, letting loose a flood of thick yellow light, the whole landscape and all the animals which roamed over its endless stretches, would become irradiated with an incandescent glory, a pristine splendour. But with the going-down of the sun all colour drained away, the earth fell under a pall of shadow, and swiftly the night would follow.

Evening was a trying time for the animals. All day long they had roamed serenely over the veldt; the gnu, the giraffe munching at the shoots of wild thorn and acacia, the high-stepping impala, the gazelle, the baboons, the vivid zebra with their fat sleek flanks, cropping the veldt grass. But with the lengthening of shadows came tension and fear. Heads kept turning, restless with anxiety. The snapping of a twig, the shadow of a bird passing overhead, was enough to start a stampede of terror. Ears were constantly listening, muzzles lifted to inquire of the wind whether death was on its way.

But once the hunting carnivores had killed the tension would let up, fear pass out of the night. This too we could see from the verandah as we sat sipping our sundowners.

Baboons frequently raided the garden but did little damage, for we had planted no vegetables or fruit. Zebras and gazelle, on the other hand, had a way of stripping the young shoots off plants and even cropping up the plants themselves, shoots, buds and all. A hyena came regularly to rummage in the dustbins, and Gushu, who kept stones in his hut for the purpose, would pelt the creature, often securing direct hits.

There were supposed to be rhino about, but the few we saw were far out over the veldt and barely discernible through our field-glasses. The only time lions came anywhere near Rose Cottage was on the rare occasions when they had killed in the forest above us, during the night. By the time we were awake and about, the hyenas had already got at the carcase, fighting hideously, and vultures, like great pear-shaped fruit, thickened on the surrounding trees.

Gushu loathed hyenas. He was a Kikuyu, and the surest way of insulting him was to say that he would die and turn into a hyena. To please him Billy went up into the forests and fired off a few rounds. The hyenas fled and the vultures took over. Gushu was more tolerant of vultures.

One morning, about four o'clock, we were rudely awakened from a deep sleep by a grunting and a squealing and the

sound of much crashing. We sat bolt upright. It sounded as if the house was being
demolished. A piece of galvanised iron
came to a grinding, clattering halt, having
slid down the steep bank below the
kitchen.

"Something is in the kitchen wrecking
it," I said, but Billy was already slipping
back under the covers.

"Probably Gushu and his *fisi* (hyena)
having it out over the dustbins," he said. I
heard the home-made saucepan-rack in the
kitchen come crashing down. More grunting and squealing and a sound like steam
escaping through a small vent.

"We'd better see what it is," I said. But
Billy pointed out that we could do no good
at this hour. Whatever it was that had got
into the kitchen had probably done its
worst by now; morning would come in the
fullness of time and reveal all.

"Get in under the bedclothes. You'll
catch your death sitting up like that," he
ordered.

But I had to find out what was going on.
Slipping into housecoat and slippers and
taking a torch I went out by the back door.
The moon was full. I did not need the

torch. Billy too had roused himself and followed me out. We were halfway along the covered passage that led to the kitchen when we saw the rhino.

It had blundered into the kitchen and could not get out again. Billy switched on the torch, illuminating the heaving flanks, the single beady eye, the profile of a good-sized male rhinoceros which, at that moment, was doggedly charging the Dover stove.

There was nothing we could do about it so we went back to bed and listened to the rhino charging about in the wrecked kitchen till dawn.

After we had breakfasted off stale bread and drunk cold milk, Gushu handed in his notice. If we didn't get a new house he was giving us the sack. As for us, we felt the same way. We had waited long enough. If Government wasn't going to provide suitable accommodation for us, we were leaving Kenya.

10

BILLY threatened to hand in his resignation. Almost immediately the Housing Committee came forward with the offer of a new bungalow in Livingstone Drive. It stood in an acre or so of garden. There were golden mimosa trees, young hibiscus, oleander and alamanda all down one side of the drive, banana trees and a few pineapples in the kitchen garden with plenty of room for growing sweet corn.

Here at last was a real home. The kitchen alone was a joy to behold, with its electric stove, pressed-steel sink and built-in cupboards. Gushu was pontifically pleased with his own quarters, walking round and round them like a bishop bestowing a blessing. He returned to report that they had running water, a good cookplace and a vegetable garden to cultivate for themselves.

What we liked best of all was the fact that at last we had neighbours near us.

We moved in. Through the good offices of friends we engaged a middle-aged French woman to act as nanny and house-keeper. To assist her we took on our staff an *ayah*, an African woman with a pleasant face and the proportions of a hippo. Gushu picked her out for us. She looked clean and held good references. In our presence he treated her with lofty disdain, but their relations in the servants' quarters were much better. In fact, though he had been collecting money to buy a third wife, he gave up the idea and purchased a bicycle instead.

We also engaged a *shamba* boy, and with his help we developed the kitchen garden with gratifying results. Our sweet corn — mealies — grew over ten feet high and produced abundantly, and the sweet pota-toes, cauliflower, tomatoes, cabbages and sweet pumpkins, though the servants helped themselves to four-fifths, yielded so profusely that there was no need to purchase vegetables.

We engaged a kitchen *toto*. But the boy, constantly cuffed by Gushu who had no time for him at all, was soon dismissed. Gushu said he was a dirty savage, but madame enlightened us on what was happening behind our backs. The *toto* had an enormous appetite, eating three grown men's share. He stole food so constantly, and in such large quantities, that even Gushu's legitimate ten per cent share was in jeopardy.

Friends called. We began to entertain and were entertained. Ralph came home from the Lady Northy. Our lives fell into a normal pattern.

But certain little incidents occurred to remind us that we were still in Kenya. There was the time I had proudly made my first hot *hors d'oeuvre* which Gushu ruined by serving all the vegetables destined to go with the meat course along with it. The meat was eaten *sans* vegetables. There was the time when he lavishly sprinkled chicken spice, bought for the purpose of making our fowls lay more plentifully, upon a dish of *coq au vin*.

But what were these compared to the rigors of Shenzi Ville and Rose Cottage?

I remember a night when we were dallying on the doorstep, saying good-night to friends who had come to dinner. Again it was bright moonlight, the mimosa smelled divine, but our friends, alas, were standing on the caravan route of a few thousand safari ants. These ants have a way of stationing themselves in the softest, most yielding parts of the anatomy before they bite simultaneously. Their bite is like fire.

Our four guests dashed past us into the house and began tearing off their clothes. The bathroom was much in demand, for the only way of getting rid of the ants was to submerge in hot water.

We began to go out on safaris again, sometimes alone, sometimes with friends. Madame was quite capable of being left in charge of the household, and Gushu assured us that while he was there we had nothing to fear.

Among our widening circle of friends were a couple called Host: he was a Dane, she a New Zealander. They were both keen safari-goers and we often formed a party and went off into the less well known territories of Kenya.

There was one particular safari I shall never forget. The rains, officially, had drawn to a close, but many showers still fell upon the high veldt and in the mountains. Benny Host possessed a fine big

American car which he had bought from a party that had come to Kenya by road, having travelled down the northern route, over the Sahara. In consequence the car was fitted with extra big balloon tyres.

All went well for the first sixty or seventy miles, but once we turned off the tarmac road and headed into the mountains our troubles began. We made for the Aberdare Range, whose two highest peaks rise 13,244 and 12,772 feet above sea level, with the rich dairy-farming 7,000 to 8,500 feet high Kinangop plateau as our night's destination.

The Aberdares are thickly forested with giants such as the Ocotea or African Camphor whose girth averages some thirty feet or so. Associated with these are other monsters such as the *Albizzia gummifera*, a graceful member of the Leguminosae family, and the *Dombeya masterii*. But so choked are these forests with under-growths, lianas and the like that it is seldom a tree-trunk can be clearly viewed. Besides, it is always dark and gloomy, even in broad daylight, within the precincts of the forest, and the atmosphere is wet, cold and dank.

At this time, though none of us knew it,

Mau Mau bands had gathered in these very forests and were being trained in the arts of guerilla warfare. It was here that they were taught how to set about killing off the white population of Kenya.

By the time we crawled up the winding mountain road what daylight there was became quenched in the eternal forest gloom. It started to rain again in a cold misty way. We switched on the headlamps. All we could make out were the black towering forest walls and dripping vegetation. There were washaways on the road which left little or no soil and which exposed the rocks under the surface. Benny's tyres, however, stood up to this rough going very well. In a little while we passed the 9,000-feet stretches and were crawling painfully through bamboo forests. By then it was pitch dark.

We hoped to reach Barry's Hotel at Thomsons Falls in time for dinner. But once we were out upon the plateau it became clear that this was not to be. The road lay a foot or two under rich red chocolate-butter mud. Every time Benny tried to move forward the car would either swivel round and waltz away into the veldt, or it would make a strenuous attempt to somersault.

The night was icy cold at that altitude and very wet. Benny tried again and succeeded only in landing the car in a ditch where it lay at an angle of 50°. If we were to spend the night in the car we had first to set it on an even keel.

Out into the mud we stepped and our feet sank slowly through six, ten, fourteen inches of cold slippery mud. I felt like a fly in treacle. It was slow work moving in that mud, for it took time to pull a foot up again — this accompanied by sucking sounds — and put it down elsewhere. Besides, every time we tried to push the car, our feet flew out from under us and the car itself remained immovably embedded.

Benny had a bright idea. He climbed back again behind the steering-wheel, started the engine up and said we were to push with all our might the moment he gave the signal. We did as he suggested. Our feet went from under us, we fell flat on our faces, and the car tyres — those great big balloon tyres — churning impotently, half buried us in mud. I could well understand the stories the pioneers told when they said their cattle drowned in mud and their ox wagons sank axle-deep in it.

Cold, muddy as we were, we had to spend the night in the car. We were on high flat tableland which stretched end-lessly into the night with not so much as a glimmer of a farmhouse within sight.

Somehow the other three slept. I listened to their gentle snores and snuffles. The only other sound was that of mud dropping back into mud. My spine turned to lead and appeared to be boring through the car seat; my neck concertina-ed into my shoulders; my head became an insupport-able weight and by the time the sky cleared and a few frosty stars pricked through, I felt as if the better part of my face had slipped beneath my jawbones and was hanging there.

Dawn came and the first thing we saw was the smoke curling up from a chimney of a farmhouse which lay hidden in a shallow valley not three hundred yards from the road. The farmer sent a tractor out. We had chosen one of the worst routes in the Highlands, he said. Having got us out of our predicament, the kind man saw to it that we came to no further mishaps until he had put us on a good sound road again.

We breakfasted at Thomsons Falls, after having washed and cleaned up. Then we went on to Rumuruti, made a circular tour and returned to Nairobi having driven round Mount Kenya. We did not see much of this mountain however for it wore a thick extinguisher of mist.

The only other incident which remains in my mind in connection with this particular safari was our encounter with a caravan of cages, each filled with wild game and destined for the zoos of the world. We were out in the scrub country beyond Rumuruti and the encounter had a flavour of Livingstone's meeting with Stanley. The white hunter in charge was so delighted by the sight of other human beings in this wilderness of thorn and sand that he stuck his hand into an ostrich cage, plucked out a handful of fine feathers and showered them on us as he bumped past. The bird was still squawking indignantly when the caravan disappeared from view.

The time came for our first local leave

and, taking Madame and Ralph with us, we went down to Shanzu Beach Hotel, where for fourteen days we did little more than swim in the shallow lagoon and laze in the sun. The following year we spent our holiday in the more spacious and much grander surroundings of Nyali Beach Hotel, but the same leisurely tempo, the warmth of the coast, the sun, the good food, the bathing and lazing made a welcome change to life on the Highlands.

Our tour was drawing to a close. We were not quite sure whether we would return to Kenya again. It became necessary to see as much of the colony as we could in the next few months.

We went on a safari to Olorgesailie, one of the recently created Royal National Parks, which lies forty miles west of Nairobi beyond the Ngong Hills and down a six-thousand-foot escarpment in the Rift Valley. This site is of archaeological significance for it is said to be the only known living-site of the handaxe man.

I remember the shock we experienced as, rounding a shoulder of the Ngongs, where up till then the veldt had undulated gently like a blown sheet, tawny green and dotted with the shade of the umbrella-like foliage of the yellow-barked fever-tree, with herds of zebra and giraffe and impala browsing in the noonday heat, we found ourselves confronted with scenery of a very different nature. The soil here was grey and bitter, with little or no grass but much out-cropping of rock. There were no trees, only different species of thorn such as the whistling thorn (*Acacia drepanolobium*) with its galls bulging along sharp spines and filled with black ants; and the giant Euphorbia standing ten, fifteen feet high, like a green and inverted candelabra. The top of the escarpment skirted a gaping void. The light beating up from the ashen soil was pallid, corpse light. We alighted to stretch our legs and adjust our senses to these new dimensions. We seemed to be looking upon the beginning and end of creation. The senses reeled before all that unlimited space.

We felt as solitary as if we alone inhabited the earth. Confronted with the boundlessness of earth and sky you become intensely aware of yourself as a human entity. You are an individual: a creature carefully fashioned by a craftsman's hands, not a thing shot off a conveyor belt at the rate of a million a minute. No longer are you an anonymity in an anonymous herd. Individuality is not submerged in the group. Something, long lost, long forgotten, is restored to you. Billy said, "Here you can lay claim to a soul."

It was then that we decided to come back to Kenya. Billy was going to accept the offer of another tour which the Kenya Government had made, and we were to return to the colony when our home leave was over.

For a long time we stood under that whistling thorn looking down in wonder at what lay before us.

Millions of years ago, during the Miocene and Pliocene periods, there occurred in this part of the world tremendous outpourings of volcanic materials from below the earth's surface. Over a length of time these outpourings built up a backbone of high ground. The Ngongs were part of that backbone. Then collapse followed collapse and through the centuries the floor of Africa's Great Rift Valley descended to its present levels, cleaving the continent in two. Millions of years from now an ocean may flow between the high escarpments that rise on either side of this rift.

Archaeologists regard the Rift Valley as a kind of tomb where the secrets of the centuries are hidden.

Our thorn tree stood on the verge of the escarpment. From here we could see a kind of "staircase" which successive faultings had produced, and which showed a succession of geological formations. We resumed our journey and dropped some 6,000 feet in a few miles along the steep walls of the escarpment. The coolness of the high veldt gave way to the heat of a sunbaked valley where dust-devils raced darkly, like waterspouts.

There were no people, no lone Masai with his spear, no Masai children tending the famous Masai cattle. We were as isolated as if we had got lost on the moon.

We had been warned to look out for rhino. We came upon a pair in the valley. It was a mother with its young one and both had their backs turned to us. At first we thought they were wild pig. Then, when we drew nearer and saw what they were, there was a scramble to get the camera out and set the stops.

Billy said he'd drive slowly past and I was to try and take at least one good shot of the two. Never before (except in our kitchen) had we been so near to a rhino. The car would have to pass within five feet of the pair.

I knelt on the seat and lowered the glass window which had been rolled up to keep out the dust. With my eye jammed to the viewfinder of our Super-Ikonta Zeiss I leaned well out, prepared to take the snap. But the moment we drew level the mother rhino turned her head, saw us, and straightway began to charge. Billy couldn't see her just then, for I was in his way.

"Keep going!" I shouted. "She's charging!"

We got away, but only just, for the Cream Bun's acceleration was not good and the rhino's horn was within inches of our rear light for the first hundred yards. In the meanwhile I had completely lost my head, sitting there like an entranced rabbit, unable to take my eyes off the rhino that was pounding behind us. The picture was never taken.

It was after three in the afternoon when we arrived at the site. An Italian showed us to one of the three *rondavels* where we were to spend the night. There were two bare beds in it, a wooden washstand, a bowl and a jug. Sanitary arrangements were left to nature — after all, there was much lonely territory about us. He gave us mosquito nets, mattresses and would have given us bedding as well, but we had brought our own.

We asked him if anyone had been to Olorgesailie recently and he said yes, four or five months ago. However, a few miles away ran the Magadi Soda-Lake road and the employees of the Soda Company could be seen from time to time driving along it. When we asked him if he ever got lonely, he smiled and said he had become accustomed to the life and was perfectly happy. Yet that man could not have been more than forty-one or forty-two years old. He had no wife with him and his only companions were two Masai and a mongrel dog.

The soil was the colour of ground-up bones, pale and supporting little vegetation. The mountains which hemmed in the valley rose gaunt and bare against a pale, soil-stained sky. We explored the ancient lake bed and saw the ancient lake levels marked by old land surfaces and shore lines. Upon the land surfaces had lived stone-age man, but these surfaces had been buried beneath successive accumulations of lake beds.

Implements of various kinds used by these ancient peoples were preserved in the tiny building above the old lake. We examined bolas stones, hand axes, the fossilised bones of prehistoric animals. But all there was of life had vanished so long ago that even the ghosts had passed away. Only a timeless hiatus remained.

As Billy and I sat under the stars that night, drinking our warm evening drinks (the ice in the thermos having melted) we could hear the Italian sitting by himself among the cactus outside his *rondavel*, playing on a guitar and singing his heart out to the stars.

And even now, thinking about those two nights we spent at Olorgesailie I seem to hear that rich, sad voice, strangely moving in its human smallness, ringing out clearly, liltingly in the vast emptiness from where even the ghosts had long passed away.

11

IN those days Nairobi was a sparkling, carefree city eagerly pressing forward into the future. The Duke of Gloucester and his Duchess had bestowed upon it new dignities, proclaiming it the First City of the British Colonial Empire. Everywhere were signs of prosperity, of growth. Here in the heart of Africa a new Britain was in the making.

But the wind, the ill wind, was blowing, blowing secretly in subterranean places, gathering force....

Africans began to pour into Nairobi from far-flung Reserves, from distant hamlets. The African population since the coming of the European to Kenya had doubled and trebled itself within a generation, thanks to the work of medical departments and a rising standard of living. Law and order made its contribution to this over-population; no longer were thousands of lives lost annually in raids, tribal warfare, ritual murders, human sacrifices.

African mortality was reduced to a fraction of what it had once been by the draining of marshland, the gradual eradication of endemic and epidemic diseases such as malaria, yellow fever, sleeping sickness, as well as infestation by various types of helminths, yaws and the dreaded leprosy.

Excellent though all this was, the balance of nature was upset. Reserves became woefully overcrowded. No longer was there enough land to go round. Fathers could not endow sons with even so much as the required minimum to plant crops and raise families.

Into the towns then poured the Africans. Nairobi being the most prosperous became the focal point of the invasion. More and more tattered scarecrows, clad in rags of discarded European clothing, jay-walked through the city, sulky, smouldering with discontent, staring into shop-windows at goods they could never buy, squatting in brooding idleness on pavements, taking note of the Europeans who to them must have seemed to possess all that an African could aspire to.

The European for his part did his own share of good work on behalf of the

African. More hospitals were springing up throughout Kenya, more schools. Private and organised African charities soothed our consciences. Our contributions were generous. Those Africans with whom we were brought in touch in our daily routine either at the Office or in the home, were recipients of much well-meant charity. On the surface, our relationship seemed excellent.

And yet that subterranean wind was blowing, gathering force. There appeared at frequent intervals reports in the paper of the beating-up of Europeans who had been unwise enough as to dally in lonely places. Disturbing rumours emanated from the overcrowded Reserves where subversive propaganda flourished. Inspectors of schools brought back reports of sedition openly inculcated in schools in the Kikuyu territories. Always it was the Kikuyu we heard about in these rumblings of discontent, and it was the Kikuyo, the tribe which had come more than any other under the influence of the European, who were stirring up trouble.

People no longer slept easily in their beds for at nights houses were robbed and damage was done to property. We had burglar-proof steel mesh put over our windows. Pole-fishing had become the vogue in Nairobi.

One night we were awakened by a small sound. Our windows were open and the night was dark with low-bellied clouds. Yet there was a sufficient lessening of darkness for us to see Billy's sports jacket detach itself from the peg on which it hung and sail across the room towards the window. We were in the midst of a visit from pole-fishers.

When Billy turned the torch on the window, two men, dressed in dark clothing, dropped their pole and the sports coat. Scrambling out from behind the oleander bushes where they had been crouching, they streaked away into the night. We switched on the light. A pair of trousers and a shirt had been taken. We examined the long dark pole. It was greased and had razor blades let into its length, so that anyone who grabbed it would have their hands ripped when the thieves jerked it away.

We reported the loss to the police, but knew very well that nothing would be recovered. These thefts were well organised. Within an hour the stolen goods would be on their way by lorry or truck to some thieves' bazaar, situated hundreds of miles away, in Kitale or Eldoret or Mombasa, or even over the border into Uganda or Tanganyika.

We asked Gushu what he had to say about all this. He wrinkled his flat nose fastidiously. "Too much dirty savage come to Nairobi now. I am afraid to go see my *rafikis* in Shanty Town because there is too much thieves there."

But into Shanty Town, as the African location outside Nairobi was called, we went, commissioned by the *Geographical Magazine* to take photographs to illustrate an article written by Richard Frost. Gushu came along as guide and behaved as if he were slumming.

The sight that met our eyes was truly shocking. Thousands of Africans were herded together, men who had won distinction in the School Certificate examinations; rough, uncouth, illiterate manual workers; prostitutes, thieves, the healthy and the diseased, children and chickens all living in conditions of appalling squalor. Hovels of mud were roofed over with flattened-out kerosene tins, all clustering together like the cells in a beehive. We photographed a family of six huddling between three walls and a roof beside a public lavatory that was overflowing into the road. And it was to these conditions that the African city worker, the clerk, the office boy, the telephone operator, the shop assistant, returned after his day's work.

We were not surprised to learn in 1953, when terrorism broke out, that these shanty towns were hotbeds of Mau Mau activities.

The Government was not unaware of what was going on or of the need to improve the African's living conditions. With what funds were available, already in the year 1949 new housing estates were springing up to ease the pressure in shanty towns. . . .

Once I had to interview an African lady who was passing through Nairobi on her way home to Uganda. She had spent the previous eight years in Britain and, after having graduated at a well-known university, she had travelled extensively in Europe. I found her refined and charming, her conversation far more interesting than that of many of my European women friends.

But where was I to take her for out little talk? The New Stanley, the Avenue, Torrs — any of the hotels, coffee houses or my Club? In those days the colour-bar flamed across their thresholds. Even intelligent Europeans saw nothing absurd in this claim to a brute superiority based solely on the shade of one's skin.

I took the lady to my home.

In August 1949 I said farewell to the *Standard* and went away for a brief holiday to Europe. Athens, Rome, Zurich, Amsterdam, Copenhagen, Stockholm and Oslo, then back the way I had come, flying once more over the Alps, across the deserts and on to Nairobi.

We spent the Christmas of 1949 and saw in New Year's Day, 1950, in Zanzibar. We had made the journey by air to this strange little Arabian island, hot, verdant and slightly sinister, on the coast of East Africa. After ten days we flew back to Kenya and finished the rest of our leave at Nyali Beach hotel. We returned to Nairobi by rail, taking the night train from Mombasa.

Billy had to make a few official safaris

from Nairobi to Mombasa and he invariably took us along with him. The journey was made my car and the three-hundred-and-fifteen-mile-stretch accomplished in two days with a break at Mac's Inn for the night.

This inn is a famous half-way halting place on the Nairobi-Mombasa road. It stands in the wilderness of the Tsavo National Game Reserve and is much frequented not only by those who make the trip between capital and port, but by sportsmen and white hunters. It was at this inn that on one occasion we met Michaela and Armand Denis. They were at that time making a film in the Tsavo district.

The game warden of the Tsavo was a Mr. Taberer, or Tabs, as everyone called him. We went out with him into the Reserve and in the space of five hours or so came upon practically all the varieties of big game that are to be seen in Kenya.

Tabs kept a pet lioness. He had found her as a cub and had reared her into a fine, full-grown specimen, as playful as a kitten and as friendly and faithful as a dog. Tabs' wife and daughter lived at the inn, but he himself camped out a few hundred yards inside the bush across the road. Iola, the lioness, lived with him.

Every night Tabs used to return to the inn to have his dinner and his sundowner. But he dared not overstay, for Iola had a way of stalking into the inn to fetch him back, much to the consternation of everyone present.

Billy wished to take photographs of Iola. Tabs arranged that he should come first thing the next morning when he would find her cavorting around with his dogs. But the next morning Billy found that the Cream Bun had developed a flat tyre. Leaving the mechanic in charge of the petrol station to look after the tyre, Billy strolled across to the camp.

When Tabs saw him walking nonchalantly, for all the world as if he were in his own garden, he nearly threw a fit. It seemed that the neighbourhood was bristling with enamoured lions, all engaged in the courtship of Iola. Tabs had spent half the night throwing thunder-flashes out of his tent to keep the brutes off. Iola of course slept in the tent with him, and was as scared as he of the lions. However, Billy came to no harm. His pictures turned out to be good and appeared as a two-page spread in *Illustrated* on November 18, 1950.

The time had come for us to pack and go away on our Home leave. But it wasn't farewell. We were returning. It was only *au revoir*.

Gushu turned down an offer of employment made by friends of ours. He had a lot of unfinished work to be done in his Reserve. He too needed a holiday. We arranged to pay him a nominal salary during our absence and with much goodwill we parted.

Madame was not coming back to us. We left her with great regret and, on her part, a flood of tears. The altitude was too much for her. Through the good offices of friends we managed to get her a job in a Dar-es-Salaam hospital. The last I saw of her she was waving one hand in a frantic farewell. The other clasped a handkerchief to her nose.

Part Two

1

THE long rains fell with abundance in the year 1951 and East Africa burgeoned forth in unwonted fecundity. It was pelting down when our ship sailed into Kilindini harbour, but again I missed the spectacular sight, for again, as on the previous approach, I was in our cabin. Ralph had caught measles. The rash had not appeared but he was feverish and had spots inside his mouth.

A child had brought measles on board and there had been time to infect all the other children before he displayed the inevitable rash. On the day before we arrived, child after child went ill, but only two other mothers owned up to afflicted offspring and demanded hospital facilities.

The rest of the children were smuggled off the ship, on to the train, and subjected to the long journey inland. When the rash showed up, the mothers of these sick children claimed it was nothing more than prickly heat. One of the children, we learned later, went blind, one died as a result of complications setting in, the rest lived to carry an epidemic that was to sweep over most of Uganda and Kenya.

The doctor in charge of the Mgonjwa Hospital came on board and confirmed that our children had measles. An ambulance was waiting outside, he said, ready to convey mothers and children to his hospital. Mothers were expected to stay at the hospital, he said, for the place was understaffed.

In the meanwhile Billy was asked to report to Head Office in Nairobi. There he would be told to which Division he was to be posted. On the quayside we parted company. There were five sick children in the ambulance, all below three years of age.

All the way it deluged down. Shutters were lowered so we could not see where we were going. Conversation was impossible because of the noise of the rain drumming on the roof. In any case no one wanted to talk; we were all too depressed.

Eventually we came to a halt. Doors opened to let in the flat white rain-light. We found ourselves outside the front verandah of a neat, newly constructed building, which we were told was the European section of the Mgonjwa Hospital outside Nyoli.

The doctor had not exaggerated when he said the hospital was understaffed. Apart from several African male servants who eyed us with extreme boredom, there was a lively plump young Italian matron. No nurses, no sisters, no attendants were in sight. The hospital was in fact deserted but for ourselves and a fourteen-year-old French girl covered with fresh chicken-pox scabs.

Our sudden descent was not at all to Matron's liking. She greeted us with restraint. Hurriedly we were allocated our accommodation. Ralph and I had a four-teen-bed ward to ourselves. While we undressed our children and bedded them down, Matron impatiently paced the veran-dah, glancing fretfully at her watch, calling to us to hurry, hurry, she couldn't spend all day with us. Like the doctor, she too gave the impression that she suspected us of deliberately contriving to spoil her week-end. "Enough now," she called. "Come out. I want to speak to you."

We three mothers were lined up on the verandah and assigned our various duties. We were to be left in sole charge of our sick children. There were no nurses or attendants to assist us. If we wanted anything we were to ask the servants, who were instructed to see that we got what we needed. As the doctor had already seen the children we must not expect him back till Monday. This was on a Saturday, the time about eleven-thirty.

"This is a funny sort of hospital," said Dotty Wilson. "Won't you be here, Matron?"

"Me? No!"

We all protested that we knew nothing about nursing the sick and were scared to be left with five sick children alone in this empty hospital.

"What you make the fuss for? Your kids have only the measles," Matron cried, glancing again at her watch.

"What nourishment do we give the children?"

She shrugged. "What they want."

Suppose, we said anxiously, they took a turn for the worse? Convulsions or fits or — well, anything might happen.

"They will not have these things," Matron pronounced. Clearly she was not possessed of much patience.

I was beginning to feel that I could wring that plump little neck of hers. "How can you say they won't have fits? Their temperatures are rising."

Matron fixed me with a bright and belligerent eye. I outstared her. "You haven't even taken their temperatures," I added.

Dotty nudged me: "Shut up. You're putting the little woman against us."

"But damn it all! This isn't good enough, Matron."

Matron took a deep breath, summoning up reserves of self-control. "You are telling me how to run my hospital?"

"All you've done up to now," I went on, hearing Ralph whimpering in the big empty ward behind me, "is to treat us as if we were an imposition. You haven't so much as looked at the children."

Matron began to swell. I had seen pouter pigeons do it too, but with feathers, not with flesh and blood. Dotty whispered that the sprightly Italian was about to burst a blood-vessel and Mrs. Dixon giggled hysterically. Matron counted ten and then began to deflate.

Without a word she turned on her heel and hurried off to a little car that was parked outside the far end of the verandah.

We gave our children doses of Milk of Magnesia. We sponged them down and tried to soothe them. In spite of the rain-clouds the ward was full of the hard flat white light of an African day. The servants said there were no curtains or blinds, so I took the dark grey cotton blankets off the other beds and hung them over the win-dows. In this grey gloom, Ralph at last dozed off.

It was time for lunch by then. I was summoned to a table set in a passage between the two main wards and found Dotty Wilson and the Dixon lady already seated. With them was the little French girl covered with chicken-pox scabs. None of our children had had chicken-pox, neither had Mrs. Dixon nor I. The French girl was not out of quarantine.

But what could we do? She was lonely and longing for company. She had a refined, small-boned face and the kind of hands and feet one associates with good breeding. There wasn't a trace of African blood in her, but because she had been born in the Seychelles she would never be free of the stigma of half-caste. We made a special effort to include her in everything we said and did.

The hospital overlooked a sea-channel with a wooded countryside rising graciously out of the swift-running grey waves beyond. Flamboyant trees flamed upon the steep banks like torches and down the cliffs tumbled cascades of blue and purple thunbergia. Small native craft plied up and down the channel, each manned by one or two Africans who sang out as they went past in tuneless ululations, wild and melancholic.

The next day was Sunday. Ralph's fever was very high and I was afraid to leave his bedside. About eleven Matron rang up the hospital. As the other two mothers were busy, I answered the phone. Gone was the exasperation of yesterday. Against a background of music her voice lilted over the wires. I caught snatches of conversation and the sound of laughter. Had I taken the kids' temperatures ? she wanted to know.

I said we had no thermometer. Did I

look for one? I was asked. I said I had looked, asked the servants, even searched her office.

"Open the eyes properly," she said crisply, "and look again. It is in my office."

She could not tell me exactly where. I searched drawers and cupboards while the sound of music and laughter faintly came through on the phone. I reported back that no thermometer could be found. She didn't seem to believe me. "Ah, you have not got the eyes," she muttered, the lilt no longer in her voice.

"When does the doctor come round?" I asked.

"Maybe Monday."

"And you? All five children have high temperatures."

She snorted with impatience. "For measles what else? First high temperature. Then rash come out and there is no temperature."

The phone clicked. Matron was through with us.

Late that afternoon Dotty Wilson's husband arrived at the hospital. Richard Wilson was a District Commissioner awaiting posting to his District upcountry.

Both Dotty and Mrs. Dixon, who had had no sleep the previous night, were resting in their wards. The French girl was asleep too. Apart from myself and an iguana edging itself along the verandah, there was no other living creature in sight to disturb the Sabbath calm. Richard Wilson looked about him, wondering whether he had come to the wrong place.

"Where's everybody?" he demanded.

Dotty came out. She looked tired and her eyes were red-rimmed. She was nearly hysterical with anxiety. Tactfully I left her to enlighten her husband.

When he had gone, Dotty looked and felt much better. Richard swore he would have a word with the Provincial Commissioner. "Now let's see what happens," she said.

Monday came and things did begin to happen. In swept a furious Principal Medical Officer. He found the hospital *sans* Matron, *sans* doctor, *sans* staff. Out he swept again.

Soon after, a fussed and humbled doctor speeded up the drive, tyres cleaving through the rain-water. Matron arrived post-haste, prim, efficient: no more airs and no more exasperation. Out of nowhere a uniformed European nurse and a Seychelles woman attendant (strongly Negroid in features) appeared and took over our duties. The hospital bustled with activity.

But one thing was clear. The three mamas must go. They had given quite enough trouble and neither Matron nor the doctor wished to see any more of them.

In the meanwhile Ralph had come out in the rash and his temperature was rapidly declining. I didn't quite like to trust him to the tender ministrations of Matron and the doctor, but had no choice.

I caught the night train to Nairobi.

Sharing my coupé was a blonde South African girl called Hazel. She told me her boy-friend was on the train and might drop in later for a sundowner.

"We met in Mombasa," she said. "He dances well and I hear he is a crack shot. He keeps disappearing from civilisation from time to time, but he isn't a white hunter. I asked him if he had anything to do with the Police but he said he hadn't. Between you and me I wonder if he could be a member of M.I.5. But what on earth is there in Kenya to interest M.I.5?"

At dusk Hazel's friend came into the coupé. He was a thick-set, powerfully built Australian with a dare-devil smile and shrewd eyes. We tried to draw him out on the subject of his job, but he evaded skilfully and told us instead of Geddi, on the coast, where excavations had revealed the existence of mysterious settlements.

Presently the dining-car boy sounded his summoning chimes. I rose, but as the train was racing at a spanking pace, lost my balance. Throwing out my arms to keep from falling, one hand accidentally came in contact with the Australian's chest.

Half-way through dinner I asked why he wore a bullet-proof jacket. Kenya was a peaceful wilderness. What danger there was came from creatures unable to use revolvers or guns.

He shrugged. "One of these days you might all be wearing one," he said lightly. "Pretty sure of it, if Government refuses to open its eyes and see what is going on right under its little nose."

"What on earth is there to fear in Kenya?" we wanted to know. He refused to elucidate. Whatever it was, this was not the time to discuss it. We did not see him again on that journey. He left the train during the night, getting down at one of the tiny wayside stations on the route.

The sun was shining in a pale blue sky when we reached Nairobi. Billy came to meet me. Never did a city look more prosperous, more confident, more secure. Along Delamere Avenue the jacarandas were in flower, and the traffic island blazed with saffron, crimson, purple and flame bougainvillaea. Familiar sights, familiar faces, met us on all sides. It was like coming home again.

Billy had his new car. We had sold the Cream Bun to a Danish couple before we left on our holiday. Catching sight of the Kikuyu flower boy and his bicycle, I asked Billy to draw up.

"*Jambo*," I called. "How are you today? Your flowers look lovelier than ever. Have you a bunch for me?"

For a second the boy stared at me unsmiling. Then his eyes slipped furtively from side to side, flicking down at the Wakamba pedlars who squatted alongside the pavement, their wooden carvings spread out in neat rows upon a rush mat; flicking towards the Kikuyu paper-seller lounging against a pillar. He moistened his lips.

"*Jambo*," he said. The greeting and the smile were forced. "I think you no come back to Kenya."

"Why ever not? It's the loveliest country in the world. I was longing to get back."

He dropped his glance, indicating his flowers. "What flower *Memsaab* want?"

I was disappointed at this greeting, but I bought bunches of gladioli and violets. "What has come over the boy?" I asked Billy as we drove towards the Norfolk Hotel.

"I've noticed that same sullenness, that resentfulness, among the hotel servants. I can't think why. They were so different six months ago."

He had already met Gushu. Was he glad to see you? I wanted to know. But Billy said that Gushu's greeting had not been unlike that of the flower boy.

We were being sent to Nakuru, the agricultural capital of Kenya and head-quarters of the 49,000 square mile Rift Valley Division. A house was waiting for us. Billy's chief's name was Molyneux, the Divisional Engineer, and Billy was to be his second in command. We could leave for Nakuru within the week.

There was a boom on. Prosperity had come to this thriving British colony. More people, more money, more goods, were pouring in. On all sides buildings, houses, factories, cinemas were rearing into the cold blue skies. Banks were erecting palatial edifices. Even the Africans we saw in the streets were no longer clad in rags. With hands in pockets, dressed flashily, spiv-fashion, they swaggered about the streets and pavements, elbowing their way through the crowds, giving place to no one.

It was in the Kikuyus who swarmed all over Nairobi that we saw the biggest change. Old friends had turned sulky, their greetings reluctant. The hotel servants, who had been such jovial, happy-go-lucky fellows when we stayed there six months ago were now taciturn; the room boys off-hand to the point of insolence. The first hint of a shadow had fallen. We sensed it but gave it no further thought.

I went back for Ralph and on the day I returned with him we set off for Nakuru. It was one hundred miles away from Nairobi and the road being tarmacadam all the way, we did the trip in under two hours. The beautiful little Italian church at the foot of the Nairobi escarpment stood more or less on the southern boundaries of the Rift Valley Division. Its northern boundaries marched alongside those of Ethiopia, the Sudan and Uganda. Plenty of scope for safaris, Billy pointed out as we flew along.

Soon we were established in a little stone bungalow set plumb in the centre of a two-acre garden. Gushu was on the doorstep to greet us. In the work involved with unpacking and getting settled in I had no time to observe him closely, but that he had changed in some subtle way was obvious.

In silence he received the presents we had brought him: the gaudiest necktie that London could sell, a wrist-watch, a spectacular ring from a costume jewellery store, two vividly checked shirts and a pair of tartan trousers.

"What did you do with yourself while we were away?" I inquired.

"I stayed in my home."

He looked half-starved. The giraffe face was gaunt. "Have you been ill?" I asked.

"No."

Evidently a diet of posho and potato-tops wasn't sufficiently nourishing. I asked after his wives. The first one had died in childbirth. The second one was no longer plump but had successfully produced a girl baby. His mother had picked out for him another good fat young woman, and as soon as he had collected the bride-price he hoped to purchase her.

"Have you any money left in your Post Office Book, Gushu?"

He shifted his feet uncomfortably. "All finished."

At that time Nakuru was a scruffy little township, huddling into a pleat of the Great Rift Valley, 6,070 feet above sea level, a mile or two from a blue, flamingo-frilled soda lake and green sloping pastures. To the west the nine to ten thousand feet high Mau ranges reared up grape-purple against the sky, austere and grand, dominating the view for as far as the eye could see. To the east rose Menangai, the township's landmark. Built upon the flanks of this extinct volcano, 7,371 feet high, was the European residential area, fine stone-built houses under red-tiled roofs, looping higher and higher every year.

Long ago Menangai had blown its top, leaving a crater 2,000 feet deep and eight and a half miles in diameter. Far back in time, no one seems to remember exactly when, the Masai had hounded an entire tribe up the slopes of Menengai at the point of their spears and pushed them over the rim into the crater below. The gradients up this old volcano are gentle and a car can make the climb in second gear.

On the first Sunday in Nakuru we took a picnic basket and drove up Menengai. Rough grasslands covered the slopes. Halfway up we saw a batch of *rondavels*. Against the vastness of their surroundings they had been all but invisible from the road below. We noticed a number of Africans congregating about them, far more than one would expect from such a small huddle of *rondavels*, but we did not give the matter a thought. The forestry department had ringed the crater with a belt of pines. The trees were young, not more than ten or twelve feet in height.

We chose a cool spot in the shade of the outer edge of the forest for our picnic. The views from here were tremendous. Below us Nakuru looked like a scatter of pebbles divided by the main trunk road, with the European quarter on the Menengai side and the Indian and African on the lake side. The lake itself was bright mineral blue, and from that distance the thousands of flamingoes wading on its shores looked like pink froth. Beyond the lake and up the wide slopes, bright green with growing grain, our eyes travelled, up and up, to high ridges and the bronze glint of great cliffs, up and up through heavy forests, up to the pristine heights of the Mau range.

The altitude made us sleepy. After lunch we stretched out upon the rugs we had brought. Ralph promptly went to sleep. Billy and I dozed off. In the noontime silence not even a bee stirred.

After a while we heard voices. I was about to sit up, but Billy signalled me to lie still. Africans were passing within a few yards of us, but because of the tall grass they hadn't seen us. The car was parked out of sight in the forest. When they had gone past and were disappearing down the slope we sat up. Brightly in the daylight, Gushu's tartan trousers glowed like a neon sign. It was his day off and he had every right to do what he wished with it.

"I wonder," said Billy, "just what they have been up to."

We watched the men diminish in size and finally disappear below our range of vision. Each man carried a *panga*, the large flat-bladed knife of East Africa. Gushu himself had one. He brandished it as he chatted with the others. What had they been doing inside the forest?

"A little *pombe* party," Billy said. Indeed those dozen or so Africans had a drunken air, reeling slightly as they swaggered down the mountain side.

2

NOT long after we set up house in Nakuru, Napoleon came to live with us. We had already acquired a black female cat from the Joneses next door.

Napoleon had been born in a packing-case on Bob and Mary Pope's back verandah, his mother being Mary's spaniel and his father an Alsatian from Snobs' Alley, farther along, who spent his time siring families all over Nakuru.

Bob and Mary brought him over to us in a rainstorm. We placed the little bundle of fur on a sheepskin rug before a roaring log fire. The cat Josephine took exception to the newcomer, and kept sauntering over so frequently to slap his face that I sat myself beside him to keep the peace. I was drinking hot rum and milk.

Dusk swiftly turned to darkness and only the leaping flames lit our little drawing-room. I noticed that my rum and milk was diminishing very rapidly even though I was only drinking it in sips. A drink that size usually lasted me till dinner-time.

"I think maybe Napoleon likes rum and milk too," Mary said.

I put the almost empty glass down and we all watched. In a few seconds an inebriated puppy staggered to its feet, got as far as the glass, thrust out its muzzle and missed the glass by inches. One unsteady paw reached forward and upset the rum. With a sigh of bliss Napoleon subsided into it, falling asleep immediately. From that day he had a little rum and milk with us when we had our sundowners.

It had been arranged before I left Britain that I should do some news reporting for the B.B.C., but after the first few reports, broadcast from London in News Reel, I gave it up. Not only did it involve chasing around after a story, but sending it down to Robert Stimpson in South Africa who would then get permission from the B.B.C. for me to transmit it. When this stage of the intricate business was reached, I had to go down to the Cable and Wireless offices in Nairobi and transmit the story from there to London, where it would be recorded.

Gushu continued to be sullen, withdrawn, preoccupied. He spent his free time squatting on his doorstep doing nothing, just staring and staring before him.

One day when I was in the kitchen kneading dough for the bi-weekly breadbake I tackled him about this. As usual Ralph was perched on the table, one crafty finger crooked inside the bowl to catch windfalls. Behind him, silent and brooding, stood Gushu.

"What's troubling you, Gushu?" I asked.

"Nothing."

"Are you ill?"

"*Hapana*. I not ill."

Was all going well back in his home? Were his children in good health and his wives and parents? All was as it should be I was told. Did he like Nakuru? He said he did. Was he sure he didn't wish to return to Nairobi? He was sure he did not.

"Then why do you go about with a face like that?" I pulled an expression of sullen brooding, eyes fixed inwards upon some secret trouble.

Nervously he moved his hands. "I okay."

"Something happened to you, Gushu,

when we were away in Britain. You have changed. You are not the old carefree Gushu we left behind. Won't you tell me what it is?"

There was a long pause and he fidgeted nervously. "I have pain."

"Pain? Where? Why didn't you tell me before?"

"My pain is too much. It is here." He tapped his head.

Misunderstanding him completely, I fetched aspirins and wrote a note to the doctor in charge of the Native Civil Hospital. I advised him to go at once and take the day off. Perhaps the pain was due to catarrh or sinus. With all this rain and the ground soaking wet, he was quite likely to have contracted something like that.

He took the note; he took the aspirins. Helplessly he looked from them to me. "*Memsaab*," he began gently. "*Memsaab*, why you come back to Kenya?"

"Take the aspirins now. They will relieve the pain." There was some freshly brewed tea. I advised him to have the aspirins with a hot cup of tea.

"Ah, no, no, *Memsaab*!" he said, sounding as if he were about to break down and cry. Without a word more, he turned and left the kitchen.

That first year I did not go away much on safari with Billy. The roads had become dangerous after the continued rains and we did not think it advisable to risk taking Ralph out upon them. I found myself spending a great deal of time on my own in the little stone house.

The house had a galvanised iron roof that made queer noises as it contracted and expanded with the varying day and night temperatures. When Billy was at home the noises never bothered me. But when I was alone at nights, I would lie awake for hours listening to the unseen feet stalking overhead, the sudden pistol-shots, the creakings and crackings, the suppressed explosions. Even in the intervals of silence I kept imagining a focusing of hidden forces up there above my head. It was with relief I would hear the feet start up again, stalking above the kitchen, pausing above the dining-room, coming nearer and nearer. . . .

One night, Billy being away, I found I could not stand the roof noises a moment longer. I rose, slipped into a house-coat, wrapped a shawl about myself and went out of the front door. Outside the moon was full, silvering the garden, glinting on the dew-washed leaves. I sat myself down on the porch in the shadow of the climbing roses that smothered its pillars.

Presently the night's soothing tranquillity was disturbed by a small sound. The snapping of a twig and no more. Along the ki-apple hedge which divided our garden from the Joneses a party of Africans came, making straight for Gushu's rooms.

I was not unduly disturbed, for the servants often entertained their friends at nights, when their work was over and they had time to spare. But what sent a ripple of doubt into my head was the fact that it was now nearly two in the morning, too late even for an African's party. When the coast was clear, I stole out into the back garden, keeping well to the shadow of the mimosa trees.

All but one window in the servants' quarters were in darkness. I crept towards this window and, standing on a stone block, I managed to peep over the sill into the room.

The room was not more than ten by twelve feet, but it was packed with Africans.

Some sat on Gushu's bed, some on his chest of drawers. On the floor in a tight circle round a kerosene oil lamp were more Africans. A *simi* or Kikuyu sword lay in front of one of the men. He had his hand upon it and was addressing the room. As he spoke in the Kikuyu dialect I could not understand what he said, but every eye was fixed on his face, and at his command one or other of the Africans would rise and come and squat before him, placing a hand on the blade of the *simi*.

I stood for a while, shivering with the cold, fancying I was looking in on some native version of a masonic ceremony. The shadows of the men grotesquely stained the four walls. The lamplight glinted on flat noses and high cheekbones and teeth bared in speech. Gushu must have been there but I could not see him, for the black faces in that red gleam of lamplight were not easily distinguishable, looking like masks, with the hollows under the cheekbones and sunken eye-sockets carved out in black shadow.

I went back into the house. If Gushu wanted to hold a Free Masons' meeting in his rooms it was his affair. I decided not to say anything about it.

The rains fell abundantly. Altogether the year 1951 was one of plenty. Faith in the Colony's future had never soared higher.

We decided to buy ourselves a house in Nairobi. We possessed a little money and argued that a house in the capital of this fine, flourishing land would be a wise investment. Every day we carefully studied the advertisements.

But property was fetching record prices. A three-bedroomed house under a tiled roof standing on an acre or so of land in Nairobi might fetch anything from £4,000 upwards. Building societies demanded that the purchaser put up at the very least one third of the purchase price.

Whenever Billy went down to Nairobi, Ralph and I went along too. Ralph was left for the day at the Lady Northy, Billy went off about his own business and I set out on a search for a suitable house.

At last I found one in a good locality, newly built, well within our means, situated near the main Nairobi-Nakuru trunk road, within convenient distances for shops, schools, bus stops. I explained my plan to Billy when we were having lunch at the New Stanley Grill Room. The house was so new that the masons were still there putting in last-minute touches. We could furnish it with our own furniture from the little stone house back in Nakuru. Government was issuing a new and rather smart-looking type of house furniture to their officials for a small annual rental. Wherever we lived from now on we could rent Government furniture. I had the Livingstone Drive bungalow curtains and carpet which did not fit our present much smaller abode. They would do nicely for the new house.

"By the time I have finished furnishing the place, all our prospective tenant will have to do is to walk in, bringing along nothing more than personal belongings, such as clothes. Everything else, from refrigerator to saucepans, crockery and cutlery, will be ours."

Billy looked doubtful. The idea of putting all our money in this one project seemed a little risky. Suppose something went wrong and we were in need of cash, what were we going to do then?

However, he came along with me and had a look at the house himself. It was structurally sound, he said, and he liked the neat disposition of the rooms. The acre and a half of garden was, of course, nothing more nor less than a hunk of untamed Africa, but with the aid of a few *shamba* boys, miracles could be worked.

He raised two objections. The whole plot lay below road level, sloping towards a central oval where, the agent assured me, the Municipality intended putting up a children's playground. What happened to the land when it rained? Just then we were nearing the close of a comparatively mild dry season.

The agent could not tell us. He said he himself lived on the other side of town. But as the house stood in a neighbourhood of brand new, very smart-looking houses, we argued that nothing too bad could happen in the district when the rains did come.

The second objection was that there was no visible demarcation of the boundaries. The bungalow stood about three-quarter way up, on the edge of red earth. It faced out upon the long rectangular acre which levelled off in the direction of the oval that might one day be a playground.

"It says an acre and a half in the plan so

it is an acre and a half you'll be getting," the agent said.

Billy went back to the office and left me to clinch the deal.

The agent seated himself behind a very big desk and I was placed in a chair opposite him. On the walls of this office were huge maps of Nairobi, Kenya and East Africa, all pricked out with glass-topped pins. While I was there, feeling reckless and fearful, the telephone rang. When it was laid down again I gathered that a £45,000 farm had changed hands. What were the few thousands we were going to spend in comparison?

"Well? What have you decided?" The agent was a busy man and had little time to waste.

"Will the owner consider reducing the price?"

"He's already come down £300. No!"

The telephone rang. The agent said acidly into it, "As it happens I have a prospective purchaser right here with me now." He listened for a few seconds, growing red and looking annoyed. "If you wanted to sell the damn thing yourself why did you bother us in the first place?"

The voice on the other end of the wire sounded apologetic. The agent said crisply, "I'll ask her." He fixed his round blue eye on me. "Well? Yes or no?"

I took a quick breath. All our savings, all the capital we possessed in the world, was about to be committed. Suppressing a shudder I nodded, "Yes."

He said something into the receiver and replaced it. He began to look slightly human for the first time. "Spring Valley is a very popular district. Houses there are a good investment."

"Spring Valley? Is that the name of the district? How delightful."

"Valley of eternal spring," he said. He typed out a letter in duplicate and pushed the sheets over to me. The letter stated that I would pay down £500 at once on the house and the balance within three months. With a bold hand, belying the creepy-crawly fear in the pit of my stomach, I signed my name.

We discussed a few more business details. He knew of a good lawyer who would act for me. As we were putting up more than the required third of the purchase price, he saw no difficulty over the mortgage. I told him we wished to put as much as possible into the house and take out the least possible amount on mortgage, for we both had a horror of debt. He thought that wise. I asked him what other expenses we should expect in connection with the purchase; lawyers' fees, for instance.

"The fees should be around sixty pounds or so," he said.

Driving back to Nakuru that evening, Billy and I found little to say. We were both committed to the purchase of a house, the little money we had was about to be tied up, and neither of us, tired as we were, felt particularly optimistic. Fortunately Ralph was asleep in the back of the car and not climbing over our necks, or trying to balance on windows, or demanding every five miles to get out for an express purpose which he would promptly forget the moment he was in the open.

"My people went bankrupt back home in Canada," Billy said gloomily. "Over property it was."

The creepy-crawly in my inside grew bigger and bigger. "We'll find good tenants, don't worry. As soon as we get possession

I'll write to the Rent Control people to call over and give us an assessment."

"Tenants! My people had tenants. Nearly drove them insane, did those tenants." We were in no mood to glory in the splendour of the sunset over the Kedong Valley or to enjoy the sight of Longonot catching its crater alight with sunbeams. We stopped at the Bell Inn, Naivasha, and had a double whisky each.

3

ALAS, the estate agent had been far too reticent on the subject of the extra expenditure involved in purchasing a house. I was soon to learn that there was more to it than putting down a deposit of £500 and providing a third of the purchase price. The first shock came when the mortgage firm sent a valuer over to look at the new house. The loan was to be based on his assessment and not, I found out when it was too late, upon the price asked by the vendor.

The assessment fell below the purchase price by £650. This left us short of the required third by some £250. Over and above that, the lawyers of the mortgage company were charging something in the region of £150 for their services. But once we had begun there was no drawing back. Gritting our teeth we paid up, scraping our bank balance down to nothing. There was yet the £60 to find for our lawyer's fees, but that we hoped to save out of Billy's salary.

We were given possession of the property on November 15, 1951. But I did not know about this until one day I happened to meet the gentleman whose house we had bought and he inquired casually how I liked living in it. He was surprised to learn that out lawyers had not informed us that we could move in.

The next step was to go down to Nairobi and get the property ready for renting to a prospective tenant. Billy did not like the idea of being left behind in Nakuru with only Gushu to look after the house and cook his meals, but agreed that, under the circumstances, there was nothing we could do about it. Arrangements were made in a great hurry, to load the furniture on a lorry, and for Petunia, our *ayah*, two *shamba* boys, Ralph and myself to go off to Nairobi for an indefinite sojourn in the new house. Billy would visit us at the weekends.

Within a matter of days we had the curtains up, the floors polished, the furniture, crockery, cutlery, and pots and pans in their proper places. But before the house was ready for viewing something had to be done about the garden.

From early morning till late in the evening the two *shamba* boys and I worked side by side on the upper part of the plot. This bordered upon the road and was about a third of an acre in extent. The soil here was good red earth, but as it sloped very steeply it had to be terraced. I visualised all that red earth cascading down and filling the back of the house when the rains came. The house lay a good hundred feet below road level.

The terracing took about a week. I bought young jacaranda saplings and planted them to form an avenue. The horseshoe-shaped drive I edged with christ-thorn, and I spent a few more pounds on bougainvillaea plants and flowering shrubs. Billy returned on the second weekend we were there and was delighted with the improvements.

"Now for the front garden," he said. "You'll find that tough going, even though the land is flat. There's all that grass."

The previous Friday a Kikuyu contractor had paid me a visit. He agreed to cut down the grass for a sum of £10. On the following Wednesday he turned up with a bevy of young Kikuyu girls who set about slashing at the shoulder-high grass with their *pangas.*

I left them working away at it, singing snatches of tuneless, wordless songs, calling to each other, exchanging remarks with some of the male servants from neighbouring houses who gathered on the boundaries to watch them work. One glance at the sky as I stood at the bus stop convinced me that the short rains were imminent. Heavy rain-filled clouds scraped their undersides along the Ngong Hills and Don ya Sabuk, the atmosphere was thundery and depressing, the light the colour of bleached bones.

At half past eleven that morning the skies ripped open and down swept a deluge. It was shortly before one o'clock when I got back to the house. Walking down the driveway with its one-in-five slope was a feat, for the surface was running with rich mud and as slippery as ice. Ralph met me on the doorstep, eyes shining with excitement.

"Come and see the lake. We have a real big lake of our own. Come and see the lake, Mummie."

With sinking heart I made my way to the front of the house. The Kikuyu contractor and his bevy were squatting on the verandah, joking and laughing with my two *shamba* boys. The contractor rose from one of the verandah chairs on which he had been seated, and came over to me.

"*Angalia! Marji mingi!*" Water lay like a sheet over the whole of the lower part of the garden. Pricking up through it were the stalks of the grass already cut. At the bottom of the garden the grass still flourished, the contractor pointing out that round there the flood was waist deep. I could see then what I had failed to notice before. Our plot was situated at the lowest end of that great oval of land, the whole district tilting towards it. Thanks to the tall grass this had not been apparent.

The Africans watched me in silence, and I tried not to look as desolate as I felt. The contractor had dug out specimen hunks of the soil that now lay under water. He showed them to me, shaking his head. Instead of the rich red earth I expected, I saw charcoal-coloured mud.

"All that black cotton. Volcanic! Very bad," he said. "You will have plenty trouble with black cotton."

I paid him off and after he had gone, taking his chattering bevy with him, I sat out on the verandah, looking over the slowly rising lake, wondering what on earth I was going to do. Ralph had discovered a spring bubbling up from under the verandah steps. With a piece of string tied to a curtain pole, he was busily fishing in it.

All our money tied up in this, a debt hanging over our heads and no more money in the bank: I could think of little else. Who would want to rent a house with a lake for a garden?

Presently the rain ceased and Petunia came out to say I had a visitor. Close on her heels followed a big-boned, largely built, elderly lady.

She said she had heard that it was my intention to rent the house and was interested. She and her family had only temporary quarters now, looking after a house for a couple who had gone to Britain on home leave. Houses were almost impossible to come by in Nairobi and she was beginning to feel desperate.

I rose and indicated the lake, the spring, and the rain which had begun to fall. "Who would want this?"

She said *she* did. And glad to have it too. When I realised she was not having fun at my expense, I showed her round the house, gave her the inventory of what we were renting with it, and told her what we were allowed to charge. The way I felt just then, I was prepared to halve the rent.

My visitor was a woman of business. She said the rent was reasonable but she was interested in a long lease. Anything under a year would not suit. This I assured her would be all right by us, for as long as Billy was in Government service, the Government would provide accommodation for us.

Next day the lease was drawn up and signed. It was the fifteenth of December; but I was so relieved to have found a tenant for Much Binding — as we called it — that I told the elderly lady she need not pay rent for what was left of the month. I rang up Billy and told him about it. He said he would come down there and then to take us back to Nakuru. Life on his own without us, he said, was becoming thoroughly tedious.

There was something else I had to speak to him about. Since the previous evening I had been visited with all manner of anxieties on behalf of my friend Mary Pope.

I could not explain why I should feel that way about her. She had seemed perfectly healthy when I had last seen her in Nakuru twelve days ago.

"How's Mary Pope these days?" I asked.

"Strange you should mention it. Mary was whisked off to hospital this morning. Something frantically serious. They're going to operate on her today."

My anxiety grew more and more acute. I could hardly concentrate on what I was doing as I cooked our last meal in Much Binding, packed our belongings and prepared to wait for Billy's arrival.

Suddenly, at about 3.30 in the afternoon, my heart lightened. All my fears on Mary's behalf were gone. I knew without a shadow of a doubt that all was well with her.

When Billy arrived I asked if he had any news of Mary. But he had left Nakuru before the operation had begun and could tell me nothing. The first thing I did on reaching Nakuru was to ring up the hospital. Yes, came the reply, Mrs. Pope had undergone her operation successfully. She was doing well.

On five other occasions dating back over

the years I had experienced a similar foreknowledge of events. How or why this was I cannot explain.

Soon Christmas was almost upon us. But that year we decided to cut down on gifts and entertaining. Our bank account had diminished to nothing and was in danger of shrinking into the red.

Gushu came running in to me one morning as I stood in the kitchen arranging flowers. He thrust out his foot and I saw the top of a ki-apple thorn buried like a nail-head in his flesh.

"Help me, *Memsaab*," he said, turning his head away and screwing up his face.

The thorn had gone deep. With finger-nail and thumbnail I caught at the head and drew it out. It was an inch and a half long, but fortunately had emerged intact, leaving no pieces behind to fester. Out gushed the bright dark blood.

I dressed the wound and bandaged the foot. Gushu thanked me, but stood sulking by the kitchen table, obviously wishing to talk. I went on with the flowers.

"*Memsaab*, you buy house in Nairobi. That is bad."

"Why is it bad?"

"Plenty trouble coming. It is bad."

"Has the trouble anything to do with these Mau Mau one reads about in the papers these days?" For about a month now, small reports had appeared occasionally in the papers concerning the activities of a sect that called itself Mau Mau. My remark was no more than an arrow in the dark.

Gushu said earnestly: "All European must leave Kenya. European take our land. When my chiles become grown up I have no land to give them."

This argument about the European taking Kikuyu land was as hackneyed as it was untrue. I pointed out to him why there was now not sufficient land to go round. Over-population, over-breeding, congestion, these had resulted from the benefits which the European had brought to the African.

"In the Reserve not enough food for us all. We are hungry. Our lands not enough."

"And the land you have, you do not look after," I reminded him. "When Government sends you officers to show you how to prevent erosion, how to make your lands yield more, what happens? You won't listen. You say he wishes you to improve your land so that he can steal it. That is not true and you know it. Why do you not trust us?"

"*Hapana, Memsaab*. Do not say that. I trust *Bwana* and you more than I trust African. *Memsaab* knows that."

"And yet you want us to go."

"I have trouble in my head," he muttered, and I began to see that it was something which aspirins couldn't cure.

"Can we not help you with your trouble, Gushu?"

He said nothing, but stood there, head bent, pinching the thorns off a rose stem with his nails. "You and *Bwana* is good. You do good for me and my wives and my chiles. You make us your *rafikis*. You do not take anything from me. You give me plenty things. You good."

"The African needs the European to help him make a good-living country of Kenya. Don't try to turn us out too soon. When I say "us", I mean all Europeans, not just *Bwana* and me. *Bwana* and I do not care to live in Kenya for the rest of our lives."

"You buy house, *Memsaab*."

I explained that the house was an investment. Money lying idle in the bank must
be taken out and made to work. When the
time came, we would sell out and return
home. Our roots lay elsewhere. Kenya, like
all those other countries we had lived in,
was no more than a stopping-place on a
long safari.

"You will go back then to your home
in Canada?"

"Yes, presently. Not just yet. Perhaps
we will not return to Kenya when this tour
is over. The time has come for us to settle
down in our own country."

"That is a good thing. Too much trouble
is coming to Kenya, *Memsaab*. Too much
trouble."

4

THE *ayah's* name was not really Petunia. It was Fatuma, but Ralph had begun to call her Petunia and the name stuck. She was a tall, slim woman, with slanting eyes, high cheekbones and a complexion much lighter than Gushu's. Being of Nilo-Hametic origin — she was, after all, a member of the pastoral, war-like Nandi tribe — Fatuma, or Petunia, treated Gushu with veiled contempt. Neither could speak each other's dialect and when compelled to converse they spoke in Swahili.

Relations between Petunia and Gushu became more and more strained, but what exactly caused this neither would reveal. I would hear them quarelling in the kitchen or in the garden outside their quarters, but if I happened to approach they would promptly cease and sulk off. All I learned was that Petunia did not approve of Gushu's nocturnal parties in his room. Once I overheard her threaten to go to the police about it.

223

"Why do you two quarrel?" I asked Gushu, when on Boxing Day 1951 Petunia gave in her notice. Either Gushu went or she did, she said.

Gushu's face was swollen with suppressed rage. But there was something else — fear, uneasiness, a furtiveness in his manner, and instead of offering a reasonable explanation he said that Petunia was a Nandi and therefore a hereditary enemy of the Kikuyu. I was not to pay attention to her machinations.

On December 28th while we slept soundly in our beds, a police raid was carried out in the servants' quarters. The next morning Petunia could hardly conceal her triumph. On the other hand Gushu became sullen, pleaded illness and stayed in his rooms. I learned later that the police had found eleven Kikuyu in his quarters, but as there was no evidence of alcohol being consumed and the men were servants from the neighbouring houses, not strangers to the district, they took no action. All they found was a battered old Kikuyu *simi*.

Petunia decided to cancel her notice, but the relationship between her and

Gushu did not improve. I gathered that from then on there were no more meetings in Gushu's rooms but that Gushu himself went out at nights and stayed away till the small hours.

"Ah, those Kikuyu," said Petunia, "are a bad lot. Always they make plenty trouble."

Canasta parties were popular in Nakuru. We were at a canasta party one night when I accepted, instead of the usual drinks, a fruit cordial which my hostess proudly declared she had concocted from a French recipe. Everyone else had stoutly refused this concoction. It was thick and looked slightly off. Billy signalled across the room to me to decline, but my hostess was looking so downcast by now that I accepted a tankard full. She said she would give me the recipe too. Of course, she admitted frankly, she had long forgotten what French she had learned in school, but it did not matter, because when making cordial she used her common sense.

With plenty of crushed ice the drink did not taste too bad. I made it last from eight to half past one and by then I felt as if a balloon was expanding inside me and sweat prickled uncomfortably out of my skin. We did not stay till the end of the party.

Out in the cold crisp mountain air, I tried to shake off the feeling of nausea. I told Billy I felt ill and he said he wasn't surprised seeing that I had been poisoning myself all evening. "You've turned pale green," he said. "I tried to warn you against the damned stuff."

Instead of driving straight home, he thought a little run up Menengai would refresh me. The moon was shining out of a clear, frosty sky. We sped down Snobs' Alley, under the archway of jacaranda trees which were in full bloom. We paused for a few minutes to look at the house we were shortly to move into.

It was old and dignified, with wide sweeping lawns surrounding it. There were graceful pepper trees silvered with moonlight, several beautiful jacaranda trees, their heavy clusters of blossom a shimmering blue at this time of night under the moon, oleander in full flower, hibiscus that threw little black pools of shadow upon the dew-wet grass. The house had only recently been vacated by a family with three children. No one was living in it just then for it was undergoing repairs and alterations.

Also the drawing-room and dining-room floors, which were old, cracked cement, were being replaced by cedarwood parquet. There had occurred a small delay in the matter of the flooring, otherwise we should have been living in that house from before Christmas.

The house being the property of Government, to the Public Works Department fell the job of making the required improvements and alterations. The work was put in charge of one of the staff, a little below the rank of foreman. This gentleman was a European called Valance.

Mr. Valance was getting on very well with the rest of the house, but when it came to the drawing-room floor a large bump caused by the rising surface near the front door was encountered. Before anything more could be done the bump had to be removed.

He called one of the African labourers and said, "Dig here." But within the hour he fell ill with malaria and stayed away a week. When he returned, the African was still digging. Even his head had disappeared from sight.

We drove leisurely on. The night was beautiful, the countryside still, wrapped in moonlight and slumber. Only the wild creatures, foraging in the night, were out at that hour: dik-dik and duiker, hare, a few snakes lying in the dust, a herd of buck. Presently we left the houses below us and were making our way through the wide grass belt.

Far across the heaving flank of this ancient volcano we could see red fires and hear drums beating where the small colony of Kikuyus lived half-way between the forested summit above and the last row of European houses far below. The distance between us and the cluster of *rondavels* was too great to see at all clearly what was going on among them, but we received the impression of a large gathering, of a concourse of black woolly heads stippling the moonlight that elsewhere lay undisturbed.

Billy drew up a little below the forest belt. "Now," he said, "stick your finger down your throat and bring up that ghastly fruit juice."

I tried. But the sensation was so horrible that I failed miserably.

"You weren't trying hard enough," Billy said. "Have another go. As long as you have that stuff inside you you'll feel pretty awful."

I tried again and succeeded. Billy's long, smooth hands were cool against my brow. Almost immediately I began to revive; the nausea was gone.

We found a rock and perched on it and lit cigarettes. The night was sharply cold but infinitely refreshing. Suddenly our attention became focused on the silvery grass farther down the slope. It was violently agitated by an animal tunnelling its way through it at a spanking pace.

In a few moments, out into the open dashed Napoleon. He must have seen us while on his nightly rounds of Snobs' Alley and adjacent streets, and followed us up here. We made much of him. He was a fine big fellow, nearly full grown, more like his Alsatian father, but with the liquid eyes of his mother, Mary's spaniel.

When we drove back home Napoleon condescended to sit with us in the car.

But once we were down again and driving along the foot of Menengai he jumped out. He was of an independent disposition and didn't care for being locked indoors at night.

The following day I had a coffee party, but was unable to enjoy it because of a feeling of over-all malaise. Christmas had come and gone. Now there were the New Year's Eve dances to look forward to, but feeling the way I did, I could not whip up any real enthusiasm.

That same night I was awakened by pains in my right side. I must have been moaning in my sleep for Billy was already awake, propped up on one elbow, looking anxiously down at me. I told him of the pain. He fetched me a hot-water bottle and began to dress.

"Where are you going?"

"To get the doctor." He would not be put off. Pain was always a danger sign and he was not taking risks.

The doctor who arrived happened also to be the Government surgeon. That is to say, he was not exactly the holder of an F.R.C.S. but he was studying to be one. He was married, with a half-grown family, looked intelligent and was efficient. I have great faith in the knowledge of the expert. When after prodding he looked extremely grave, I pressed him to tell me the truth. It was better to know the worst.

It turned out that he wasn't absolutely certain. It might be acute appendicitis. It might be worse. I recalled Mary Pope's operation. Mary had said: "They removed everything. I nearly died."

"If you are not better in the morning," he said, "we'd better open you up and see."

Morning came and the pain was, if anything, more acute. The doctor came again, prodded and knuckled. He decided to operate straight away. When he had gone back to the hospital to make the necessary preparations, Billy, who was white in the face and looked far worse than I did, wanted to know if I had told the doctor about the fruit cordial. He was certain that all the trouble was due to my friend's unfortunate concoction. Of course I had not mentioned the drink.

The grapevine was at work. Friends heard and within the hour were calling at the house, walking on tiptoe, speaking in undertones. An atmosphere of leave-taking shadowed the sunny morning. Ralph was brought in to kiss me good-bye. He was to live with one of my friends while I was away. Petunia was going along too.

"What's going to happen to my Mummie?" Ralph demanded, tearful and obstinate. "Why can't I go with her?"

Petunia shook her head, fatalistic and resigned. To use the knife on the human body was a bad thing. She saw little hope for me. But why worry? To everyone the end must come. Being of a brave and war-like tribe, she bade me brave to the end. "*Shauri ya Mungu.*"

Gushu broke into a fever of activity. He dragged all the drawing-room and dining-room furniture into the garden, he took down curtains, he began to work with a zest he had not shown for many a day.

"You get well and come back, *Memsaab*," he said sternly, making a face at the departing Petunia behind her back, muttering at her. "That Nandi is a fool. You hurry and get well. I will make the house shine for you. You will say, 'Gushu, you are a good boy. My house you make to shine,'

Don't be afraid for *Bwana*. I will cook his food very good. Don't be afraid for anything. The European doctor is clever, not like our witch doctors. You hurry and come back."

He carried my suitcases to the car. He closed the door. He pointed to an untidy flower-bed which I had tried for days to persuade the *shamba* boy to dig over. That bed would be dug and planted when I got back, he said. He would plant and dig himself.

The last I saw of our house was Gushu standing under the porch waving a duster.

It struck me that this might be the last time I would look upon the bright blue lake with its frill of flamingoes, the last time I'd see the grape-purple mountains and the jacarandas in bloom. The last time I'd hold Ralph in my arms or share with Billy the fun, the adventure, the happiness, that had been our lot from the day we first met, so long ago now, in India. We knew each other very well and above everything else had become great friends. I longed to tell him that the years of our marriage had been the happiest in my life and to thank him. But these things, even in the moment of farewell, are difficult to put into words.

We drove in silence under the avenue of jacarandas, swung up the hospital drive.

"It's that damned fruit juice," Billy cried indignantly. "There's nothing wrong with you. Only wind."

5

I PUT myself trustingly into the hands of the experts. When the nurse who prepared me for the operation had given me the injection that was to lull my fears and send me into a state of preliminary unconsciousness, I showed her the sterilised Kilner jar I had brought along. That was to hold whatever the surgeon removed, I explained. If I survived, I felt entitled to see what had caused the trouble.

"Take your teeth out," she said, ignoring what I had said. But my teeth are my own. She left me to enjoy the pleasant sensation of drifting away into unconsciousness. My anxieties dropped away from me, my fears were gone. Much Binding and the lawyer's bill, which I awaited with sinking dread, were no longer of any consequence. Away and away and away I floated.

But, alas, the effect wore off and I was awake to a sharp-angled actuality by the time they were ready to operate. The nurse returned accompanied by two African attendants who wheeled a stretcher alongside my bed. The nurse was preparing to roll me gently on to the stretcher; but this wasn't necessary; I stepped over myself and settled down, hiding the jar under the blankets. Nurse and attendants looked nonplussed.

I was wheeled along corridors and covered ways. Faces appeared at the windows and it occurred to me how much idle curiosity a corpse was spared on its last journey. Those who recognised me waved and I waved back until the nurse said I was to lie still and do no more waving.

Mary Pope told me that she had been only partially conscious when she had been wheeled into the operating theatre, but what she saw when she got there was so terrifying that she promptly swooned away. When I made my entrance I felt as if I were in a film set and the nurses in their white robes, the surgeon and the anaesthetist were actors got up for the part. It put me in an objective frame of mind and made me more than a little self-conscious, for here was I the centre of all this fuss.

In order not to cause anyone any bother,

when the stretcher was wheeled alongside the table, I got up once more and stepped over, settling myself down again. The Africans giggled and wheeled away the stretcher. The rest of the room eyed me in profound silence.

"Remove your teeth," said one of the theatre nurses. She couldn't believe they were really my own and had to make sure. The surgeon went over to a wash-basin under a window, and scrubbed assiduously, but I saw him eyeing me the while.

It was time to produce my jar. I placed it on the trolley which had been drawn alongside the table. The trolley was loaded with glass and chromium objects. I explained to the surgeon that he was to be sure and put whatever he removed into the jar. The surgeon nodded once and continued to scrub furiously. In his white robes he no longer cut a dashing figure; he looked bulky, epicene and comically pregnant.

One of the nurses tucked my hands under my spine, another drew woollen socks over my legs. The anaesthetist showed me a large glass tube with a long needle at one end and a plunger at the other. He explained that he was going to give a jab with the needle and I was to start counting — one, two, three. . . .

When consciousness returned I was back in my room and a nurse sat beside me. Seeing me awake, she at once unhooked a gadget that had been fixed under my tongue.

For a little while I savoured the thought of being alive. Then I remembered the jam jar. Where was it?

"We'll talk about that later," the nurse said. "Relax now and sleep."

"What did they remove?"

"All in good time. The doctor will tell you."

Something had gone wrong with my eyesight. It was like looking through fast-flowing water. I drifted off again. Full consciousness did not return till late in the evening, but I knew that Billy had visited me and sat by my bed.

That night was a difficult one; I gave a great deal of trouble which I wished I could have avoided. But feeling as if I were a corpse already filling with gases, I was sick off and on until well into the morning. And all the time I lay awake I heard the sounds of revelry floating gaily through the cold African night. It was New Year's Eve and at midnight rockets went off and bells rang in the year 1953.

A fear that had lain at the back of my mind took possession. What had they removed? I was too young to have cancer, but still ...

A warm, liquid tongue licked my hand. A friendly head thrust itself against my wrist. Napoleon had come to share that very difficult night with me.

He stayed with me until morning, dodging under the bed whenever the nurse came round. Then, having bitten the African who came to replace my flowers, he was caught and dragged out by the collar, a compact, indignant hunk of dog, his paws sliding over the polished floor.

Billy called morning and evening. There was a gleam in his eye which made me very suspicious. I knew that gleam from of old. He told me that we were now moving into the house in Snobs' Alley and that Gushu worked as ten men. We must do something about giving him another salary increase.

Gushu himself came to visit me. I recognised the Joneses' choice roses wrapped up in brown paper, but it was no time to look a gift horse in the mouth. He had taken pains with his toilet, adding to the bright tartan trousers and yellow shirt a new purple coat, white-rimmed dark glasses and a trilby.

"They cut you, *Memsaab*?" he asked in awe. "Did it hurt?"

When I sat up to arrange the roses in a bowl, he quickly snatched them back, looking wildly scared. Lie down, he said. I must lie down. Even though I explained that the stitches were reliable, he would have none of it. The moment I complied, he said "*Kwa heri*" hurriedly and all but ran out of the room.

My surgeon visited me, but briefly. He would not stop to talk and ignored my pointed references to the jam jar. Even the nurses pretended a profound ignorance. This conspiracy of silence only made my fears more acute.

Then Billy told me. The gleam in his eye was by now a positive bonfire. It seemed that though the doctor had rummaged upstairs and down, he had found nothing at all wrong with me. Even my appendix, which was in a very healthy condition, was too small to catch hold of.

"I told you," said Billy, "that it was only wind. You should never have drunk that fruit cordial."

Five days before I was due to leave hospital Billy brought me the lawyer's bill. We never opened each other's letters, so he had no idea what was inside that long envelope. I did not tell him either.

The bill amounted to £343, and we had only £9 in the bank.

How they had arrived at that figure I am still not quite certain, though I have the statement before me now, neatly typed out upon blue paper. As far as I could make out, my lawyers felt entitled to charge exactly the same fee as the mortgage company's lawyers. This on top of their own fees, the stamp duties and so on! Also there had been some correspondence, which came to nothing, over the boundaries of the property.

Napoleon had become an established visitor at the hospital. He arrived after a good dinner and did the rounds of the surgical and maternity wards while the nursing staff were occupied over the change from day to night shifts. By the time the night sister came twinkling along with her torch, he was sleeping peacefully under my bed.

That night I was grateful for his company. Every time I moved he was sitting up beside my bed, his nose thrusting into my hand, his ears warm and velvety to the touch. By morning I knew what I must do.

It was not right to expect Billy, with his fixed salary, to find the £343. Besides, in the first place it was I who went ahead and bought Much Binding. In days gone by I had taught myself shorthand and typewriting, seeing them as necessary to the career of a journalist. There was a shortage of stenographers in Nakuru and the salaries offered were indeed high. But my shorthand needed brushing up.

Morning came and in the apocalyptic stillness I watched crimson and yellow wash over the sky, tinge the Mau escarpment with a blood-red glow, turn the lake into a sulphur pit. The *vlei* burned luridly in tones of reflected scarlet and gold. Even the birds, the flamingoes snaking high in long loose formation, the pelicans and storks and sacred ibis, catching the dawn fires upon breasts and outspread wings, looked as if they had been dipped in blood and sulphur. But when the sun came up the colours softened and the new day rode calm and open of face, with only the gentle tints of a soap-bubble to brighten the sky. In Nakuru, mornings came with grace.

Napoleon's reputation had become a byword among the African staff. Reluctantly one of the attendants showed up with the flowers, circling the walls and eyeing him as he lay with his muzzle resting on his front paws under my bed. The servant placed the flowers on a table and was backing out when Napoleon did an almighty dash, showing his teeth. He didn't so much as touch the African. There was no need to, for his reputation alone was enough. The man screamed and ran. Napoleon prudently made his exit.

Shortly after nine, when we were resting after all the tidying up and straightening out that goes on in a hospital in the morning, I had a visitor. The pretty blonde South African called Hazel who had shared a coupé with me nearly two years ago dropped in. She said she was employed as a receptionist in an hotel up Molo way, but had strained some hip muscles while riding. She was much better now.

We talked of her Australian friend who had worn a bullet-proof vest and had mysteriously left the train at one of the lonely wayside stations during the night.

"Funny you should mention him," said Hazel. "He dropped in only the other day at the hotel. He said that any moment now the balloon will go up. Apparently this Mau Mau we read about is a far more serious matter than any of us think. He said that Kikuyus are pledging themselves to kill at least one European each. As there are millions of them and only a few thousand of us, he foresees a wholesale massacre. Unless, of course, something goes wrong with the Mau Mau arrangements."

Hazel was leaving Kenya anyway. It was not, she protested, because of what her Australian had said, but she was getting homesick for Cape Town.

"You British don't know how to deal

with the nigger," she said. "You behave as if the nigger thought and acted and had the same beliefs and environment as yourselves. You've got him thoroughly confused. He likes to be told what is black and what is white. All these half-tones only bewilder his simple, savage mind. Now as for us South Africans. You take my word. When trouble breaks out there, no South African will be touched. The niggers have a healthy fear of us."

Billy brought me, at my request, an old shorthand text-book I owned. For the rest of my stay in hospital I swotted up shorthand.

Five days out of hospital I got myself a job as stenographer in the P.W.D. It was however only temporary, for the regular stenographer was away on sick leave and would be returning in a month's time.

Fortunately for me, most of my dictation came from Billy. He was very patient and spoke so slowly that it would have saved time if I had taken down his letters in longhand. My typewriting was faster and I was able to deal with the work that came in for typing from the rest of the department much more efficiently.

Billy still did not know the reason for my sudden desire to do office work. I wished to spare him the knowledge for as long as I could and until I proved by my own efforts that I could pay the lawyer's bill. In the meantime I had written to the firm, explaining the position and asking them if they would accept payment by instalments. No reply came, so presuming that there was no objection, I sent them my first month's salary, which was £35.

At home, in spite of Gushu's improved attitude to his work, he and Petunia rowed continuously. One day she took the firewood chopper to him, chasing him round the *shamba*. I returned from the office and was informed that she was leaving there and then.

I paid her off, wondering how I was going to look after Ralph and keep a job at the same time. But hardly had Petunia disappeared round the gate than Jessie was produced.

Jessie was a comely Buganda woman, plump as a pea, neat, clean and mission-educated. Her references were good. With only a twinge of misgiving I employed her. It was against my better judgement that I left Ralph in the care of an African *ayah* at all.

Right from the start she and Gushu got on like a house on fire. Obviously she had no tribal prejudices, like the puritan Nandi Petunia. In fact she had so little prejudices at all that in no time a gap was cut through the back fence — the servants' quarters were some three hundred yards or more away from the main house — and the men servants of the neighbourhood began to queue up outside the gap. But this I did not learn till later.

Before my time ran out at the P.W.D. I applied to and was taken on by the Kenya Farmers' Association. The salary here was in the neighbourhood of £45 a month. Billy could not understand why I insisted on keeping on with a job. It was unnecessary, he said. My place was with Ralph.

I felt that the time had come to break the news.

We were sitting out on the front verandah of that old, picturesque, rambling house in Snobs' Alley. Dusk was deepening into night and through a filigree of bare jacaranda branches and twigs — the dry season being well in by now — stars were pricking out one after the other. Ralph was asleep. Gushu sang to himself on the kitchen *stoep* while his food cooked on the Dover stove. We accorded him this privilege of using our kitchen to prepare his meals because he said that when he cooked in his own rooms he had to share his food with his *rafikis*, who had a way of dropping in at meal times. At this hour too, fat and giggling Jessie would be sitting on her doorstep like a tabby cat, while outside the fence her admirers began to queue. Africans wasted no time on courtship. They asked straight away about terms.

We loved this quiet evening hour, with its tranquillity, and the sound of voices crooning distantly in the starlit dusk. Feet resting on pouffes, drinks at hand, we'd watch the lights coming up across the *vlei*, the weaving of headlamps along Millionaires' Row, the night train with its rows of lighted carriages, slowing down before entering Nakuru railway station.

Billy heard me out. When I had finished he made only one comment. Whatever happened I was not to overdo things. I had not got back my full strength yet. I must not tire myself.

We decided to cut down our expenses wherever possible. Our monthly bill at Karim Bux's, where we bought groceries, vegetables, drinks, crockery and in fact everything we needed, stood in the neighbourhood of £50. We would stop entertaining and explain our reasons to our friends. Usually I spent a great deal of money on foodstuffs — cooking expensive continental dishes, serving wine with dinner. From now on a diet of potato chips and eggs — eggs were cheap in Nakuru — and local fruit in their seasons, *sans* wine, *sans* fresh cream, *sans* other expensive delicacies, were to be our lot until the debt had been paid off.

"We'll reserve to ourselves this one consolation," Billy said, indicating our sundowners.

Working at the K.F.A. meant rising early in the morning and covering the distance between our house and the office on foot. As I began work at 8.30 a.m., and Billy was not due in his office till 9 a.m. and he had the car, I saw no reason why he should be dragged out of a morning to ferry me to my job. Gushu prepared a piece of toast, which I ate when I was sitting behind my desk in the Stenog's Pool. At lunchtime Billy called for me. The moment I got home I'd set to and fry our potato chips and bacon and eggs — a diet varied twice a week by meat dishes, and once a week by spaghetti — then after a hurried lunch go back again to the office, Billy giving me a lift. When Billy was away on safari, I'd stay on at the office, consuming the sandwiches I had brought along, and leave little Ralph in Jessie's care, praying that she would not starve him.

Apart from all this, I had taken up writing in earnest again.

I would wake up at four o'clock in the morning, sneak off to the dining-room which was a corridor and the width of the drawing-room away from our bedroom, and there with the aid of hot coffee out of a thermos flask endeavour to write love stories for magazines.

It was the dry season. The veldt grass withered to straw, water ran out of the lake, leaving the white powder-fine soda bed to glare sightlessly back at the sky. The flamingoes and the pelicans and the ibis and the cranes flew away in search of water. The afternoon wind raised armies of dust-devils hundreds of feet into the air. When the drought is particularly bad Nakuru becomes a dustbowl. Soda dust blows over the town, sometimes hanging suspended, making the air as opaque as a November pea-souper in London. Traffic up and down the main street often had to come to a dead stop, visibility being reduced to nil, until the dust cleared. It was a trying season for everyone, and our nerves were sorely strained.

The newspapers were now printing accounts of Mau Mau atrocities under 36-point headlines. African bodies, mutilated, bearing the Mau Mau mark of seven small cuts in the flesh, were appearing mysteriously on roadsides, in the gardens of houses, in market places. Yet no one seemed to know how they had got there or who had done the killing. We were beginning to ask ourselves if we were not taking this sect that called itself Mau Mau too casually.

Night after night fires broke out upon the Highlands, fired by unseen hands. Vast tracts of valuable forest were destroyed.

Ever since squatters had lived on Menengai the old volcano's slopes regularly broke into flame in the dry season, fires eating along the towering bulk of it, hanging red wreaths and glowing festoons against the night, and smoking rings in the day-time. Fire-breaks kept the flames from the houses at the bottom and the pine forest at the top.

Nakuru's large gardens became the haunt of buck and duiker and dik-dik, of strange birds, of soft-bodied furry creatures, refugees from the burning veldt who came to lick along drains and gutters for the rare and precious drops of moisture. Down too from the burning grass slithered the puff-adders, settling themselves in the dry flower-beds, the parched lawns, even in houses.

Those who could afford it went holiday-ing at the Coast .. . .

6

GUSHU produced a telegram, purporting to have been sent from his home. He said he must leave at once, but I was not to worry for he had found a good man to replace him temporarily. He said he would not be away more than two weeks; which meant we might not see him again for another six months.

These last few weeks had brought about a change in him. He had become absent-minded and nervy. He was still sullen. When asked if anything was wrong he would shake his head and say he had a big pain inside it. Sometimes his eyes were so bloodshot that I wondered if he had been drinking too much *pombe*. Before he left he asked for his Post Office Savings book — in which he had put money again since my return — and withdrew every cent.

The Kikuyu who replaced him, in spite of the good references he produced — no doubt borrowed from a *rafiki* — was a skinny, middle-aged man with grizzled hair and a face so thin that it looked as if it were a living skull. His eyes had fallen deep into the black cavities of the sockets, glittering there between half-closed lids. It was obvious from the start that he had never done any housework before: he would not touch a broom or wash a plate. The kitchen *toto* was hustled into doing his work for him and was often beaten when he tried to dodge it.

Toto moved through the house with the delicacy of a bull in a china shop. He broke things, he spilled and he splashed. When one of my precious Gouda urns was knocked down, I thought it time to remonstrate.

The new man's name was Kapata. I sent for him and told him that from now on he was to do his own work and that *toto* was not to be given duties outside the kitchen.

"I teach *toto* housework," Kapata said, the glittering eyes fixed malignantly upon me. He made no secret of the hatred that burned inside him.

"Not at my expense."

Kapata said something in his own dialect, shrugging his bony shoulders. When he went back to the kitchen I heard a crash. He must have deliberately tipped over a tray-load of crockery.

Jessie then tiptoed into my study. "*Memsaab*, I do not like that Kapata. Every night he goes down to the *Bondeni* (African quarter) and some nights he and his *rafikis* walk down to the lake shores. They kill cats and goats and make bad magic down there. Kapata says soon every European in Kenya will be dead."

She confessed that she lived in terror of the man. If he knew that she had told me about his lakeside activities he would surely kill her. Some nights Kapata came back with blood upon him which he would wash off in the servants' bathroom. All the other Kikuyus were afraid of him. He made them swear to become Mau Mau.

"He say he is a general," she said.

Unfortunately I did not take Jessie seriously. But I told Billy about it, and he, being a man of peace, also felt that Jessie was merely trying to get rid of the old man. All her talk about killing goats and cats seemed very far-fetched to us then, who in our ignorance were not aware that these animals were slowly and painfully put to death during the oath administration ceremonies of the Mau Mau.

"Pay him a month's wages and send him away," said Billy. This I did the next day.

I rang up the office and said I would be an hour late. It was better to wait until Kapata was off the premises before I left home. If I anticipated trouble, I was relieved to encounter none. He snatched the notes out of my hand and turned away. He didn't want any references either.

That night someone set fire to the fence which divided our garden from the Allens'. It was a wattle fence and, as no rain had fallen for two months, blazed away merrily. Fortunately our neighbours saw the fire, rushed out, and were in time to save the better part of the fence.

When Wynn Allen came round to tell me about the fire next day and I had inspected the damage, it occurred to me that for all we knew murder might be done in the servants' quarters. Neither Billy nor I heard a whisper about the fire.

"These old houses," said Wynn, "are death-traps."

There were four of them, all about thirty or forty years old, built on concrete piers which lifted the floor two or three feet above the ground. The woodwork had begun to show traces of time, and the walls, not being of brick or stone, were inflammable. A match set to petrol spilled under the floorboards, and there would be no stopping the fire.

Gushu arrived that day. When I returned from the K.F.A. in the evening, I found him sulking on the doorstep. He looked as if he had undergone a serious illness. The skin hung on his bones, his eyes were feverish, and he avoided all conversation with Billy and myself.

Slowly but surely our debt was being paid off. Our Karim Bux bill had been whittled down to £12 a month. The famous London publication *Illustrated* had printed some of our pictures of Treetops and their cheque for £50 went a good way towards easing the pressure of the debt. Gordon Makepeace, editor of *Outspan*, published two or three of my articles, with photographs. His cheque, too, was sent off to the lawyers. Unfortunately my literary efforts in the fiction line seemed to be getting nowhere, but thanks to the encouragement of Dorothy Daly, of Messrs. Curtis Brown, the literary agents, I kept at it. When the debt stood at £63 I received a letter from Dorothy to say that she had placed a story of mine with a Tower House publication for which I would be paid £75. Immediately on the heels of this came another acceptance. A London editor was offering 250 guineas for a serial I had sent him.

And so at last the debt was paid up and we were free to breathe again. I left my job at the K.F.A. after due notice, and settled down thankfully to be a housewife once more.

The rains came. The lake filled. Once more the earth became green, flowers bloomed and life was happy.

Napoleon had accorded himself the freedom of Nakuru township. He knew every byway and short-cut. When I walked to Mass of a Sunday morning, he would accompany me, lead me through the quickest ways. His insistence on hearing Mass might have turned out to be a distraction, but the African vergers, after being severely bitten, pretended not to see him curled up in the aisle beside me.

He killed deer down by the lake. Once three Africans chased him round the golf course to deprive him of a dik-dik he had brought down, and once he pushed his nose into a wild beehive and was stung so severely that his face swelled till he looked more like a St. Bernard.

The new Assistant Commissioner of Police moved into the house next door to us. We lived between the Allens on one side and the police bungalow on the other. Next to the police bungalow was the house invariably allocated to the Principal Medical Officer of the district.

While having tea with Celia Griffiths, the A.C.P.'s wife, I was asked if I had any Kikuyu servants. It turned out that many housewives were getting rid of their Kikuyus and replacing them with servants from other tribes. Celia said she had done so herself. It was too risky, under the present circumstances, to keep Kikuyus.

At about this time Ralph began campaigning for a sister. He is the kind of little boy who goes on and on persisting till he gets what he wants; so at first we took no notice. He would bring the matter up at all hours, his blue eyes wide and pathetic. He would rattle off the names of friends who had baby sisters. He would say he was the only one he knew who hadn't.

This went on until Billy and I began to wonder if we were being selfish in deciding to limit our family to one. In years to come would Ralph hold it against us? Soon we shrank guilt-ridden every time he mentioned other boys' baby sisters.

One morning at breakfast, while Billy was doing his best to read the paper, he was conscious of Ralph standing mutely beside him. For a while he ignored him, and kept on reading. Ralph sighed gustily a few times until, unable to bear the strain of the sad blue eyes fixed on his face, Billy lowered the paper to ask what was wrong.

"Pat Phillips has a new baby," Ralph said.

Billy's nerve gave. "Now look here, son. No more talk of babies. I am too old to put up with babies pattering all over the place. Never mention them again."

Two days later we gave a barbecue at which there were many guests. The weather was perfect, the moon full. Our guests were in the drawing-room, filling up their glasses before going out on the lawns under the jacarandas. On such occasions Ralph was permitted to make a brief appearance, just to say good-night and go back to bed.

The little pyjamaed figure duly made its entrance. He made straight for Wynn Allen, with whom he had struck up a firm friendship. What he said to her we don't know, but in a lull of the conversation we heard Wynn ask why he didn't tell his daddy to write for a baby sister, seeing he needed one so badly.

Everyone was intrigued. In the silence that followed Ralph's little voice piped up: "My daddy can't have babies. He's too old."

I think our daughter Ann-Marie began her existence that same night. . . .

7

MANY employers of Kikuyu servants had begun to ask themselves whether it was prudent to keep them on in the face of what was happening. For the first time the word "terrorism" was used and no longer could the Europeans of Kenya regard the murders, the arson, the wilful damage to stock and property with Olympic calm.

The time had come to have a little talk with Gushu. What did he really know about Mau Mau?

"I don't know anything," he said sullenly.

"They are killing their own people." I showed him a report in that morning's paper which stated that eighteen freshly murdered Kikuyu corpses were found in a ravine in Nyeri — a thickly populated Kikuyu area. Each corpse had been brutally mutilated. Mau Mau symbols were deliberately left along with the bodies so that there would be no mistake about who had been responsible.

"You always said there was 'plenty trouble' coming to the Europeans in Kenya. Is this the start of it?"

He shifted nervously, torn perhaps between conflicting loyalties. Trouble was coming, he said, plenty trouble.

"You go away, *Memsaab*. Go back to Canada. If Bwana will not go, you and Ralphie and the baby to come, go away. To stay in Kenya is bad."

As long as Bwana remained in Kenya, come what might, I said, we would stay by him. Gushu heard me out, shaking his head. He reverted to the old cry: there was a pain in his head. Bad magic was making plenty of trouble in his brain.

"Would you be happier if you left us, Gushu?"

He raised his hands and let them drop. *Hapana!* He would stay on. But if I wished — and I was to be sure and not give out that he had advised me — I might send away *toto* and the *shamba* boy, both Kikuyus.

"Do you think you could get on with members of another tribe? Remember what happened with Petunia."

But Gushu shrugged listlessly. He didn't care. I was to get who I liked. The pain in his head was too much.

Wynn and Archie Allen owned two senile Sealyhams, to which they were devoted. Morning and evening they could be seen patiently trotting the creatures out, with Napoleon, who adored Wynn, very much in attendance. What attention he paid the Sealyhams was entirely disinterested, both animals being long past a marriageable age.

Napoleon's social activities extended beyond the Allens' home. Apart from being a familiar figure in town and an ardent churchgoer (how loud were his yawns during the sermons, which were always in Swahili at the early Mass), he also dropped in regularly at the European hospital. By the time my notice was drawn to this, he was on good terms with the nursing staff and got on well with everyone but the Africans.

One day he was led back home on a leash with a note from Matron saying that though his sympathy and interest were appreciated, she felt that perhaps he might be carrying things a shade too far when he climbed into bed with the surgical patients. I apologised and promised to keep Napoleon at home.

This he loathed. I chained him up — on a long chain be it admitted — under the jacarandas. He moped. He looked the picture of depression. His yawns could be heard up and down Snobs' Alley. Once when a few thousand safari ants dared to lay a trail across his limited piece of territory, he flew into a rage and chewed up the lot. The moment he was released off he would dash, in a tremendous hurry to catch up with his social rounds.

That would be the last I'd see of him until he was brought back on a chain with a note from Matron explaining that though he was intelligent and charming, the surgeons didn't take kindly to his supervision in their wards.

When I despaired of solving this problem Napoleon involved himself in a homeric fight with a puff-adder and got his mouth and forelegs badly bitten. The snake was killed it's true, but the poor dog nearly died as well. We hurried the vet, Mr. Brown, to him. He was given the necessary injections, and the wounds were cleaned and dressed. For days he lay in a coma. His friends called on him, the sisters from the hospital rang up to ask how he fared, Wynn visited twice a day. The first intimation of his recovery came when he had one of Jessie's admirers treed on the kitchen table. She had sneaked him into the kitchen to eat up the remnants of some left-over pie.

For the first time we heard Mau Mau news on the B.B.C. news bulletins. Gushu heard too. He looked dazed and a little flattered. "They speak of Mau Mau in Ingland!" he said, not without pride.

We engaged a house at the coast, but Gushu refused to accompany us. He wanted to return urgently to his home, he said. We took along his second, a Kipsigi called Kimanau, and, of course, Jessie. Napoleon was left to Wynn and our new *toto* had instructions to fetch Napoleon's ration of beef from the butcher's every day and leave it with her. If *toto* was left to feed the dog, Napoleon would have starved and the boy would either have pocketed the money or eaten the meat.

The journey was made by car. We took Jessie with us and left Kimanau to go by train. From Nakuru to Diani Beach it was about four hundred and thirty-five miles. We broke our journey at Mac's Inn for the night and then went on early the next morning.

Diani House was a delightful rambling building standing at the top of a five-acre tropical garden that sloped down to a white beach. The sea sand was like table salt, being, of course, composed of pounded coral. Sheltering behind a twenty-foot barrier reef, which in low tide showed through the water, was the lagoon, silky calm, flowing with the colours of a peacock's tail. Upon the reef the great breakers of the Indian Ocean crashed and crashed again with the noise of an express train that never goes by.

Casuarinas and coconut palms marched along the bottom of the garden, holding it away from the encroaching sands. When the tide was exceptionally high, waves lapped round their roots. On the rising slopes of the garden — the house stood some two hundred and fifty feet above the sea — were great bowers of bougainvillaea, camellia bushes with dark glossy leaves and white flowers, alamanda, flamboyant and thunbergia. Birds of many varieties made themselves at home on the lawns, especially the hoopoes. Swallows had built under the eaves and in the evenings when Billy and I sat out on the topmost terrace we'd see them swinging in the champagne-tinted light, cutting patterns against the jade-green sky.

We swam, we lazed. Ralph was in a seventh-heaven of delight, but Kimanau and Jessie were not altogether happy. At first they complained of the heat. Never had they known such heat. Then it was the monkeys that made free with what-ever fruit they could lay their greedy paws on. Kimanau said one even grabbed a banana from his hand at the very moment was popping it into his mouth. The mesh over the windows was not only to keep out monkeys. Nightly, leopards prowled round the garden and padded across the verandah. Jessie swore she heard them sniffing under her door.

The servants were terrified of the sea. Here was strange water indeed, never still, never silent. The tides were sheer witchcraft. A war was going on between land and water. Did I see how the waves reared up like demons, how they crashed and chased up the sand, trying to gobble away the earth? The reef was a living thing. How it champed! How angry it was! How it bared its great gleaming white fangs!

They thought we were unduly imprudent to go swimming. Kimanau and Jessie bathed at the well. But Jessie was the bolder of the two. At least she went as far as sitting herself on the casuarina branches at the bottom of the garden.

From her perch she would eye the fishermen poling along the lagoon in their dug-outs. If a large fish was caught, up she'd get, clap and call. The man was ordered to bring the fish to the house at once. Why any of the fishermen obeyed her we never could work out, but within a few minutes of leaving the sea the fish would be flapping on our doorstep. The fishermen asked ridiculously low prices. I remember paying three shillings for a three-pound crayfish.

We shared the fish with the servants. They were terrified of the crayfish and the crabs — these, too, arrived on the doorstep very much alive and in fighting trim — which gave Ralph a chance to chase Jessie and Kimanau round the *shamba* with crayfish and to put crabs in their bedding.

We were blissfully out of touch with the world. The radio set had broken down. No newspaper was delivered in this remote area. Our nearest post office was ten miles away at Ukundu. For a month we lived peacefully, happily, on the fruits of the earth and the harvest of the sea. I began my first novel, *Tides of Zhimoni*, setting it in the very scenes about me.

On our return to Nakuru it was with astonishment that we discovered that Mau Mau was still rife. In fact, we were assured, it had grown by leaps and bounds. It seemed we were *surrounded* by Mau Mau. Reports of killings, of maiming of cattle, of destruction of property appeared daily under banner headlines. Prize cattle belonging to European farmers were hamstrung, horses' legs broken, flocks of sheep and goats maimed.

The sinister part of it all was that no one knew who was friend, who foe. Trusted Kikuyu servants were proving themselves to be sworn killers. Billy came home with the news that five of his best Africans, all Kikuyu, had turned out to be leaders in the terrorist organisation.

Gushu returned to us. When I asked after his wives and children he shrugged indifferently. Everything, he said, was changed. He was bewildered. He was lost. The old tribal order had gone and there was nothing but this new chaos, this new fear, to take its place.

"If they carry out their threat," people were saying, "and every Kikuyu kills one European apiece, we'll be wiped out, overnight. They outnumber us by five or six dozen to one."

The signal. That was what we dreaded. Who would give that signal: and when?

Suspected Mau Mau leaders were rounded up and gaoled, awaiting trial. But the atrocities did not stop; in fact, as if in defiance, they became more numerous, more widespread. Up and down the rich valleys of the Aberdares, in the Kinangop, around the fertile shores of Lake Naivasha, wherever Kikuyu tribesmen lived, terrorism flourished.

The time had come to part with Jessie. Mary Pope told me of a Polish lady called

Anna Soukulska who would like the job of nanny to the new baby as well as housekeeper. Anna was living on a farm in the Kinangop. The farm was — like most Kenya farms — fairly large — 18,000 acres in extent. It was lonely and the continual raids upon the farmer's cattle, the burning down of his pyrethrum factory, the maiming of his racehorses, had begun to make her nervous. Besides, she was a Roman Catholic and wished to live where it would be possible to go to Mass on Sundays.

I had a talk with Jessie. It transpired that she nursed a secret ambition to be a seamstress. She had been collecting money, she said, and could afford a sewing-machine and the rent of a shop, but she didn't know how to sew. The women in Uganda wore Mother-Hubbards run up from brilliantly printed fabrics. If I would teach her how to cut out and sew up these garments, she could return home and set up a shop in her village, making a lot of money into the bargain.

My sewing-machine was new, but Jessie was an intelligent woman and her hands had been trained by missionaries to handle things delicately. Also I had grown fond of her.

While Jessie sewed on the back verandah, I sat out on the front verandah, typing away at my novel. It was the dry season again. Once more the lake was dry and dust-devils swirled over Menengai, over the lake-bed. Puff-adders came down, and duiker and bushbuck and dik-dik licked in the gutters for water. One night we saw a puff-adder outside the garage when we were returning from a party. Billy ran over it, but didn't kill it. The next day while Jessie sat sewing I heard a blood-curdling scream. It seemed that Jessie had felt something nuzzling along her calf and thought for a while that it was a cat's tail. (Josephine had produced three kittens — This, That and The Other.) When she looked down eventually she saw the scaly body of a good-sized puff-adder by her chair.

It must have been the snake we had run over the previous night, for it looked bruised and Napoleon made short work of it.

On Octover 3rd, 1952, Mau Mau killed the first European. Characteristically they chose a woman. Margaret Wright was done to death on the verandah of her farmhouse in the Thika area.

On October 5th, thirty-three head of prize cattle were discovered with broken legs.

On October 18th, fifty-odd African workers were killed on a European farm.

On October 27th, Eric Bower, a Kinangop farmer, was butchered in his bath. The men responsible were his own Kikuyu labourers whom he had refused to send away when warned by the police to do so. He had said he trusted them.

The headlines grew bigger. The B.B.C. now regularly reported stories of loyal Kikuyu chiefs and headmen done to death by terrorists. The Kenya Regiment was called out, and the 4th (Uganda) Battalion of the King's African Rifles entered the Colony. The assassination of loyal Senior Chief Waruhiu proved to the Colonial Office in London the lengths to which the Mau Mau were prepared to go in their campaign of terrorism. Police posts were burned down, African constables done to death. European children cut down while they played in their own

274

front gardens. The Mau Mau, being sworn to kill at least one European each, found it least risky to discharge their obligation by slaughtering children.

The Nyeri Polo Club, where earlier that year Prince Philip, watched by the Queen (then Princess Elizabeth) had played polo, was burned down; 300 acres of grazing land belonging to two European farmers in the area were fired, stables were set alight and the racehorses in them roasted alive. Mau Mau hunted in gangs ranging in size from twenty to three hundred. They entered the homes of Europeans: through the good offices of the servants — usually Kikuyu long resident with the family, and therefore trusted and far above suspicion.

The list of atrocities grew daily. The Mau Mau had it all their own way — killing, destroying, and escaping capture by melting into thin air. Where would they strike next? we asked ourselves. We bought automatics and revolvers. We carried our weapons to parties and we slept with them under our pillows. We sat down to our meals with them on our laps and in the evenings placed them where they could be picked up and fired within the twinkling of an eye. The Mau Mau attacked, we were told by a woman who had not only survived the attack (this being the first time the terrorists experienced a reversal) but had shot down several of her attackers, "like leopards springing at you. There's no time to think".

Billy wore his revolver tucked into a holster under his arm. He is slim and tall and the tell-tale bulge hardly showed. But my figure, now heavily pregnant, was not built for carrying automatics. However, carry one I must, so I hid mine in a secret pocket in my skirt which my smock concealed. Every time the baby kicked, the gun wiggled. Billy took me away to lonely places and made me practise shooting, seeing to it that I became quick on the draw.

It was a trying time one way and another. Furniture in drawing-rooms was rearranged so that no one need sit with back to door or window. Constantly radios would be turned down so that people could hear if anyone was moving outside on the gravel. For the same reason we developed a habit of breaking off a conversation to listen.

Two visiting journalists from Britain

took up residence in our guest house. We saw little of them; they were always away. One of them was also a photographer. One day he showed us pictures he had taken after Mau Mau had raided an African settlement. Smoking ruins and mutilated bodies lying where they had fallen, children slashed but not killed outright, pregnant women left to die after their bellies had been ripped open and the living foetus snatched from the womb — those were some of the things he had photographed.

When, we asked ourselves, was the signal to massacre be given?

Napoleon was chained at nights to the railings on the front verandah, from where he could have an unrestricted view over the *vlei*. He loathed being chained, but we were not going to allow him to run loose over Nakuru with all these Mau Mau about.

One night — shall I ever forget it? — we were roused by his bark. We listened. He became excited. In a few seconds excitement gave way to delirium.

We acted immediately, automatically. For some time now we had planned what action to take if we were attacked. In a matter of minutes little sleeping Ralph was carried and tucked inside a built-in linen cupboard which was immediately locked and the key hidden. Friends knew where to look, should we fail to survive the attack.

The servery and the kitchen we could not defend, but the dining-room door was locked and barred, so was the drawing-room door and the door which led from the corridor into the back verandah. I slipped a handful of bullets into my housecoat pocket. The windows were all stoutly meshed with steel burglar-proofing. The vulnerable point was the study door which opened out on to the front verandah. That was where we made our stand.

Napoleon stopped barking and began to grumble to himself. We waited, peering out of windows for any sign of Mau Mau. Bright moonlight lay tranquilly upon the lawns, silvering the peppers and the jacaranda.

We went out on the verandah with the intention of coaxing Napoleon indoors. He perked up again, pointing his nose at the hedge about three hundred yards away. Up came his ears. Gripping our guns we followed his glance. Something was definitely moving in the shadows.

We waited, holding our fire until the object or objects came within range.

Five seconds later Wynn Allen emerged into the moonlight brandishing a golf-stick. She had heard "Nappy" barking and, fearing that Mau Mau had set upon him, she had rushed out to defend him. Wynn is not quite five feet two inches tall and is of slender, almost fragile build.

Napoleon was so astonished to see first us and then Wynn, that he calmed down. When Wynn came over — the senile Sealyhams waddling in her wake to sniff under the grass blades on our lawn — he leaned his head against her, looking up with eyes aswoon with adoration.

"Let me catch Mau Mau try anything with you," said Wynn, fiercely swinging the niblick, "and I'll give them something to think about."

At that moment a saucy little female mongrel pranced across the lawn. Napoleon forgot us and went mad once more with excitement. She, and not Mau Mau, had caused the trouble in the first place.

8

THE post of Divisional Engineer, Rift Valley Division, fell vacant and Billy became the new D.E. He came home in the middle of the morning to tell me. Think of the safaris, he said. The Division covered an area of some 49,000 square miles. After baby was born and I was fit to travel again, he was going to take me everywhere with him.

Ralph's birthday came round, and Mau Mau or no, we had a rousing party for him. He was very pleased with life but a little impatient. How much longer, he asked, must he be kept waiting before his baby sister arrived?

In the meanwhile the number of Europeans killed by Mau Mau began to rise week by week. People we knew, perhaps chatted to in Nakuru's shops one day, were never seen again, having been slaughtered during the night. In January of the new year our friends the Rucks were murdered.

We all knew the Rucks; they came regularly to shop in Nakuru and at Christmastime I had talked to Esmé when she was buying presents for her African labour. They had a son called Michael, a blond little boy of Ralph's age. She said they lived in a state of siege upon their beautiful farm not many miles away in the North Kinangop.

On the fatal night Roger and Esmé were sitting in front of the fire, reading and listening to the radio. Little Michael was upstairs already asleep. There came a knock on the door; the African *syce* had come to warn Roger that something suspicious was taking place in the cattle *bomas*. Not suspecting that the man was in league with the terrorists, Roger opened the door and went out. Immediately he was set upon and hacked to death. Esmé, revolver in hand, rushed to his rescue. She was cut down, but by no means mortally wounded. Leaving her where she had fallen, the men dashed into the house, some to hack and slash and destroy everything in it, some to break into Michael's room. They had to burst open the child's door first. He had beautiful eyes. They gouged out both eyes, cut off his ankles and wrists, and then left him there to die.

Waking and sleeping I kept hearing the cries of mother and son: Michael crying out to Esmé and Esmé calling out to her child. Who had died first? Whose voice had gone on crying out into the darkness, in pain and loneliness, waiting for death?

Ann-Marie was born prematurely. She came with little fuss and was a good baby right from the start. But back in my room, exhausted as I was, I tried to keep myself awake, hand tucked under the blankets, holding my gun, for fear my baby would be taken from me. The hospital had been built on modern, spacious lines at a time when it was not necessary to put steel mesh over the great windows. The nursing staff was totally inadequate to put up any sort of resistance, should Mau Mau attack. Why they never did I cannot imagine. Patients, nurses and new-born babies were sitting ducks.

Napoleon, as a matter of course, took up residence in my room. No one tried to turn him out. No African would enter it, for his ferocious manner alone put the fear of death into them.

Ralph and Billy called frequently, both delighted at the arrival of a girl. Ralph was all for taking her away at once.

Gushu never called and I had the idea that the presence of other Kikuyu in the hospital kept him away. To show concern and interest in a European at this time was not prudent.

Anna came to us and what a blessing she was! At once she took charge of the baby and the house, and ruled the servants with a rod of iron. She was small, middle-aged, and fierce of eye. The kind of discipline I had never succeeded in establishing with the servants, Anna achieved as a matter of course. The Africans went in fear of her, though I never heard her raise her voice. Even Gushu was careful not to get in her way.

She baked delectable Polish breads, she taught me how to make "bortsch" with beetroot and fresh cream, she replanted the garden and her strikingly gorgeous flower schemes became the talk of our friends.

One day Gushu asked me where Anna came from. He made sure first that Anna was not around when he asked it, his awe of her being truly great. I produced an atlas, turned over to the map of Europe and showed him Poland. Gushu could read English. He studied the map long and solemnly.

"Po-land," he observed, "is next to Roosha."

"They are very much alike, the Poles and Russians."

He looked startled. "*Hapana!* Rooshan is black man's brother."

"Then *Memsaab* Anna is your sister."

I could see what was going on in his mind. Cherished delusions were falling apart. *Memsaab* Anna was a strict disciplinarian, unlike the kindly, easy-going, friendly "Breetish". What if the "Rooshans" were the same? In the end he borrowed the atlas and took it away, to show his *rafikis*, he said.

All Kenya was not afflicted by terrorism. It was only in the areas where Kikuyu predominated. Billy discovered a Home — like the Lady Northy — in Kitale where it was possible to leave Ralph, Ann-Marie and Anna while we went away on safari.

Kitale, 6,250 feet above sea level, centre of the rich Trans Nzoia, about 155 miles from Nakuru, was very much of a frontier

284

town. On the west was the 14,140 feet extinct volcano, Mount Elgon, dividing Kenya from Uganda. To the north, below two tremendous escarpments, stretched the deserts which eventually ended on the shores of the Mediterranean; to the east was broken terrain, precipitous mountains rising thousands of feet above deep gorges and lost valleys. In Kitale's streets, men from the deserts and the mountains, carrying spears, heads covered in mud skull-caps, and wearing hide cloaks, wrist-knives and ivory knobs screwed into the flesh of their chins, loped cautiously along, staring into shop windows. Several of the Trans Nzoia farmers belonged to the British aristocracy. This mingling of Stone Age man with the twentieth century was perhaps the town's most striking feature.

Our safaris took us to the Marun basin in the Suk district; to Maralal where the Samburu, a lion-hunting tribe, roamed over wild, mountainous country tending their cattle and living very much as they had done for centuries past; out into the deserts; to the shores of Lake Rudolph; to Lodwar which stands on the banks of the Turkwell river, a desert outpost which always put me in mind of a setting for a Foreign Legion film: to Lokitaung in the very north of the forbidden Northern Frontier district, where no white woman is permitted to live; along the boundaries of Ethiopa and the Sudan.

By now we had made up our minds that we would not return to Kenya, so it became necessary to make a record of our safaris. To do this we bought ourselves a 16-mm. Paillard Bolex ciné-camera, filming game, tribes and scenes as we went along. Billy had a safari truck for his use. We had to carry everything we needed, from petrol and water and foodstuffs to tents. In the "chop" box there would be flour, onions, fat, tinned foods. We carried pots and pans. I became expert at cooking game, taking along the necessary accompaniments to, say, roast francolin or gazelle. A favourite form of cooking was to enclose the trimmed and washed bird or animal in greaseproof paper and seal this in a plaster-cast of flour mixed with water. Roasted under a slow fire, the results were entirely satisfactory. One of Billy's young South African engineers — and who knows better than a South African how to feed sumptuously when on safari ? — showed me how to make safari bread. From him I also learned other practical tips which made our excursions into the wilderness comfortable and enjoyable.

No matter where we were, in the deserts of the north, in the high cold mountains of Maralal or Kapenguria, I always took along a model nylon cocktail gown, easily washed and uncrushable. Having washed off the dust and the grime of the journey, it was sheer delight to get into this dress and sit down to a table covered with a white tablecloth (with clips to keep the cloth from blowing away when necessary) and to be served by Muresa, Billy's safari boy, who would be rigged out in *khanzu* and cap.

I remember on one occasion being present when the pay truck accompanied our little convoy out into the desert. In the N.F.D. one always travelled in convoy.

The P.W.D. kept in repair a road which linked the outposts of Namaraputh, Todneyang, Lokitaung and Lodwar with the frontier town of Kitale. It was the only road over that part of the Northern Frontier District. The tribe here is the Nilo-Hametic Turkana, scarcely touched by civilisation. A few members of the tribe were coaxed into forming road gangs, but there was little or no work for them to do. The road in fact was almost indistinguishable from the surrounding desert; it was quite easy to mistake what might seem to be the road and discover later it was a path scoured out by a dust-devil. The dust-devils, in this region of midday mirages, of giant ant-hill cities silent as the valleys of the dead, can be fantastic.

The Turkana cannot count. Money does not mean very much to him. The road gangs were paid mainly in kind — tobacco, salt, sugar, etcetera. But they did receive money as well, East African shillings — nothing else would do — piled in little stacks on the accountant's table. Always when the pay truck halted by a road gang out would come the table and two chairs, one for the accountant, one for his assistant.

When the tobacco and so forth had been doled out and the coins placed in stacks on the table, a stack per man, the leader of the gang would step forward, a notched stick in hand. He would measure the height of each stack, making sure that they were all the same. This rite performed, the stacks would be distributed among the men.

The shores of Lake Rudolph are shallow at its northern tip. The lake stretches roughly in a north-south direction, is 185 miles long and covers an area — almost entirely desert — of about 3,000 square miles. It has no outlet to the sea and is shrinking rapidly, becoming increasingly more alkaline. There is sufficient similarity between the fish in Rudolph and the fish in the Nile to indicate that at some distant period of time river and lake were connected.

On one occasion a visiting V.I.P. from Britain, accompanied by Billy and another highly placed Government official, drove off across the desert — we were all staying in the *boma* of Lokitaung twenty miles away— to inspect the boundaries between Ethiopia and Kenya. Rudolph had shrunk out of Ethiopian territory, well behind the Kenya border, leaving no lake at which the Ethiopians could water their cattle and goats.

Having done with their inspection, and the combination of the bright desert sun, the glaring sand and the heat being overpowering, they decided to go for a swim in the lake. The water looked inviting enough.

When, in the company of the rest of the party, the truck I was in came within hailing distance of Todenyang, an agitated young official raced towards us in a Land Rover. We were to halt right there until further orders.

It turned out that the V.I.P. and our other two gentlemen had stripped, stepping briskly into the lake in the expectation of finding themselves waist deep within a few feet. Fifty yards from the shore the three had begun to hurry; a hundred yards and they were running, still ankle deep in Rudolph's waters.

Maralal is a big game area. Whenever we went out there we never seemed to have brought enough film to photograph the elephants, the lions, the herds of ibex and kudu, the teddy-bear-eared Grevy's zebra. When the time began to draw near for us to leave Kenya, one of Billy's young engineers offered to shoot me a Grevy's zebra so that I could have its hide as a souvenir. These zebra have a finer stripe than the zebra of the Highlands.

The animals in these lonely tracts of the north are unafraid, inquisitive and almost friendly, particularly the zebra. The young engineer indicated a fine herd of them and asked me to pick out the animal whose hide I wished to have. This was impossible because they all looked alike, but he fancied a plump specimen in the forefront of the group.

Just as he was about to shoot, that same zebra came trotting over, large dark eyes fixed inquiringly on us. He came to within fifteen yards or so, head a little tilted, eyes full of curiosity. Of course it was not possible to shoot such a friendly creature. Gladly I gave up all hope of possessing a zebra skin.

We went on safari into the famous game district about the Narok area. This is Masai territory, a hundred miles from Nairobi, a hundred miles from Nakuru travelling westwards over the undulating high veldt. I expected to find primitive warriors and lion-hunters, but film companies often passed that way and the local Masai were as camera-conscious as film stars. The picturesque specimen I singled out to film insisted on a careful briefing as to what he was expected to do. When I explained this, and obtained his approval, he paced out the area where he was to perform his little piece, rehearsed three times, and when he was satisfied, ordered me to "shut".

These safaris relieved the nervous tension under which we lived. Then Billy and I decided to spend our local leave on a tour of the Congo, Uganda and Tanganyika. We travelled 1,800 miles in four weeks, visiting out-of-the-way places and making films. We saw the Mountains of the Moon; we saw the famous lakes, George, Edward and Albert. When it was possible, as at the lovely mountain resort of South-West Uganda, Kabali, we had a few rounds of golf. The Mufimbiro mountains appear spectacularly soon after leaving Kabale. It was a clear cold day when we first saw them, and the puffs of smoke above each fuming volcano were tinged with red. We lived at various points in the Belgian Congo. We saw the pygmies and watched the Watusi doing their famous dance. By the time we reached Tanganyika we had run out of film.

We returned to Nakuru very tired but very satisfied with all that we had seen and done. The thought that these scenes, these places, would soon be beyond our ken, made the whole safari particularly significant.

Christmas came and went. The year 1954 was ushered in at an unforgettable dance at the Golf Club. I can't remember when I had enjoyed myself more. Mau Mau was still with us. There had been the terrible Lari massacre when three hundred loyal Kikuyu were butchered. There had been other atrocities, but now, gradually, the tide was beginning to turn. No longer did the Mau Mau have it all their own way. The doomed European was fighting back. Up on the high Kinangop, in the Aberdares, about Naivasha and under the snows of Mount Kenya, farmers engaged in running battles with the terrorists, and even when hopelessly outnumbered, drove them away. Casualties among the raiders rose sharply. The township of Nakuru itself remained singularly free from disturbances. But all around us, within sight of Nakuru, up Rongai way, up along the sloping pastures of the Mau Ranges, in Solai, Sabukia and Gilgil, the terrorists were still active.

They were running short of guns and ammunition. Houses were raided while

THE MAU MAU

WANT *YOUR* GUN !

SEE THAT THEY DON'T GET IT

IN THE LAST THREE MONTHS 65 FIREARMS HAVE BEEN STOLEN FROM PRIVATE INDIVIDUALS

19 WERE STOLEN IN MAY
28 WERE STOLEN IN JUNE
18 WERE STOLEN IN JULY

EVERY ONE OF THESE IS A
POTENTIAL MURDER WEAPON

GUARD YOUR GUN

their occupants were away, for the sake of obtaining firearms. Gangs began to operate along the lake shores. They baffled the police, each man seeming to possess the power to vanish into thin air after a raid. Where did they come from? people asked. The suspicion grew that these men, the terrorists' trained desperadoes, were the Fifth Column. Were they the servants and the artisans and the clerks who could be seen going about their daily work under the protection of their employers?

Evidence of oath-taking ceremonies was coming to light in our midst — on the heights of Menengai, on the less-known stretches of the lake shore. Remembering Kapata, we realised that he must have been one of the ringleaders, an oath administrator, rallying the Kikuyu of the district under the Mau Mau banner.

Some of the Kikuyu who had been forced to take the oaths were harmless enough. The old servant at the P.W.D. who made tea for all the European staff openly acknowledged being a member. He said men had come to his house one night, held a *panga* to his throat, led him down to the lake shores and there compelled him to swear to kill at least one European. If he hadn't taken the oath, the old man said, the others would have chopped him up. He had seen what they did to men who opposed them.

I didn't like the idea of him making tea for the P.W.D. staff. It would have been too easy to slip in some poison. I even tried to coax Billy to put him on another job, but that, said Billy, would hurt the old man's feelings and prove that no one trusted him. Up to the day we left Kenya, old Musea went on making tea for the staff and helping himself to three-quarters of the sugar and tea ration.

One night we heard the splutter of distant gunfire. We left our beds and rushed to the window. A farmhouse at one end of the lake appeared to be on fire. It made a small red glow upon the vast slopes of the distant hillside. Next day it was confirmed that terrorists had raided and fired that particular farmhouse, and the place being made entirely of timber, blazed up like matchwood. By some miracle, however, the occupants had managed to make their escape unharmed.

Again no arrests were made. For days the

whole area was combed, the Army and the Home Guard helping the police. Not a trace of the phantom attackers could be found. Yet according to eye-witness reports, the gang had numbered over fifty.

That morning after the fire I found Gushu fast asleep in the drawing-room. He was in a sitting position, his head lying against the window-seat. He had dropped off in the midst of polishing the floor.

When I spoke to him, even shouted, he didn't hear. His face, which had fined down to the very bone, was corpse-like with exhaustion. Eventually I summoned Kimanau to wake him up.

Gushu opened bloodshot eyes. They were dull and uncomprehending, as though his brain still slumbered. Without a word he staggered to his feet and blundered out of the room. We did not see him again until the evening.

Much Binding fell vacant as our tenants were leaving the colony. They said they could not stand the strain of living in Kenya any longer. As we ourselves were not returning, there seemed to be no point in hanging on to the house.

But since the beginning of the Mau Mau

troubles the prices of house property in the affected areas had dropped alarmingly. Accommodation was as short as ever in Nairobi and houses were still much in demand. But very few people were willing to invest in house property at that time.

I went down to Nairobi and together with an estate agent looked over Much Binding. The structure of the building was sound enough and had stood up to a succession of rainy seasons. But the walls were spider-webbed with small plaster cracks which were enough, said the agent, to turn any prospective buyer — should he find one — against the house. The paintwork on the steel-framed windows was blistered and peeling off, the walls and ceiling in much need of redecorating. The jacarandas on the rising slope above the house had grown from six-inch plants to twelve-foot trees. They had to be thinned out, for they had become a young jungle. Again the grass was waist-high along the large apron of ground in front of the house and, said the agent, must be trimmed down, for who would want a snake-pit on his doorstep? The worst fault of all was the drive. It curved steeply down from the road above in a horseshoe to the kitchen door. The rains had worn gullies in its surface and part of it had already been washed away. The tenants had not possessed a car, so the state of that drive had not worried them unduly. Before the agent would even consider placing the house on his lists I had to put that drive in order. It must be metalled, he said.

Very depressed, I told Billy what the agent had said. Billy promised to write off to the appropriate people who could do all that was needed at Much Binding. Only two of his letters were answered. Both firms said that as most of their Kikuyu labourers were now in detention camps it was impossible to take on any more work.

"What are we going to do?" I kept saying. The house was empty. In its present condition the agent doubted whether he could even get us a tenant. We were eager to sell it. But who would buy property in such a poor state of repair?

Billy's hands were full at the time. He worked late into the night and was seldom at home. Prisons were needed to house the Mau Mau convicted of terrorist activities and detention camps were springing up in far-flung, inaccessible parts of the Division.

"Let me go down to Nairobi. I'll take Anna and the children, Kimanau and two *shamba* boys. I'll take Napoleon too," I said. "You know what a splendid watchdog he is. If you will arrange to let me have two painters to work for me, I am sure I could get Much Binding shipshape again."

Billy wouldn't hear of this. The Mau Mau were daily growing bolder, daily more desperate. The children and I were safe here in Nakuru. In Nairobi no one was safe. A gentleman we knew there was attacked one evening while walking round his garden with his dog. A housewife had been hacked to death by a vendor who had been selling her eggs and fruit for the past ten years. Another housewife had opened her door to a man wearing the uniform of the Electric Company who said he had come to read the electric meter. He turned out to be an assassin.

I was not to mention the matter again, said Billy. Let Much Binding take care of itself.

But this I couldn't do. It represented our capital. We were going to need that capital when we left Kenya. Again I tackled Billy.

It was the occasion of one of our rare rows.

Weeks passed. We had reached an impasse. Much Binding hung upon my consciousness like an obsession. At the risk of another quarrel I tried again. This time at least I was heard out in silence. There really was no other solution. Even Billy saw it. If he could have taken some leave — and he was not due any — he would have come down to Nairobi himself to share whatever perils awaited us at Much Binding.

Eventually I wore him down. Reluctantly, much against his better judgement, he took us down to Nairobi. He also gave me paint and brushes and two of the best African house decorators in Nakuru. When the time came for him to leave us and return home he very nearly changed his mind and hustled us all back with him. "God only knows whether I'll ever see you again," he muttered. But, of course, Billy was always a pessimist.

9

NAIROBI was tense. People walked in fear. Mothers took their children with them wherever they went; the day when a child could be left to the care of African *ayahs* was gone. Most of Nairobi's housewives went out to work in offices, in shops, in banks. The cost of living in Kenya was high and families counted on the wife's salary to help out. It had come to a stage when working mothers even took their children to the office with them.

A woman walking down the road, fifty yards from Much Binding, was set upon and beaten up, and the men got away with her revolver. She wore it too openly in a holster on her hip.

Anna was delighted with the move. Her daughter, married to an Englishman, lived in a beautiful house nearby, and Anna could visit her often.

Napoleon at once set about discovering the possibilities of Spring Valley. He ranged far and wide and I never saw him except when he returned home at dusk. The servants I had brought along with me, including Kimanau, had never lived in a big city before. It was not the thought of being surrounded by Mau Mau that worried them. Nairobi's swift-moving traffic sent them into a trance of scandalised terror. For the first few days they would not cross a road unless Anna or I led them, and then only in the manner of a flock of desperate chickens.

Two days after we had taken up residence in Much Binding, Billy came to see us. He had left Nakuru at seven that night and arrived on the doorstep at nine. He spent the night with us and was on the road again at five the next morning. He threatened to keep this up until we were safely back home with him.

Ralph and Ann had the time of their lives "helping" me. They started to decorate the kitchen themselves when my back was turned, emptying a pot of hard gloss enamel on the tiled floor and succeeding in getting the cabinets, the stove and the sink well plastered with it before they were discovered. It took days to remove the paint off the furniture, and a week to get it off their skins. The rains were not quite ended. Off and on a shower would fall. They were heavy enough to turn the bottom of the drive into a quagmire of red mud and Ralph and Ann had wonderful times making mud pies. I found quite a few of these in the refrigerator. The mud being red and virulently staining, children and house were never free of it.

The agent called. By now the house was looking very spruce, in spite of the children's attempts to help. The garden had been tidied up and the *shamba* boys were mowing down the waist-high grass with their *pangas*. He agreed that if the drive was put in good usable condition he saw no reason why he should not fix us up with a reliable tenant. As for selling . . . ! He didn't advise it — unless we were prepared to let the property go at half the price we had paid for it. Did I not know, he asked, that Spring Valley did not mean "valley of eternal spring" but *valley of a hundred springs*?

Early the next morning, while his mother was preparing breakfast, a four-year-old boy in Spring Valley was butchered in his own front garden, the body left where it had fallen on the tricycle.

Billy arrived before midday. He was in no mood to argue. Anna and the children were returning at once to Nakuru with him. And so was I.

I couldn't agree to going back at that juncture. My work on Much Binding was nearly complete. Only the drive remained to be done. We argued for an hour. I begged for four days' grace. If in that time the drive was not yet completed, I would go back to Nakuru. If it was done before the end of four days I would telephone him and he would come and fetch me at once.

Again I won.

Billy drove off at three in the afternoon. Hardly had I waved him out of sight than a Kikuyu contractor stopped on the road-side to talk to me. He indicated the drive. In poor shape, wasn't it? What was I going to do about putting it right?

He was neatly dressed, this man; he had a clean, intelligent appearance. I had seen him supervising some workers who were laying out a drive farther along the road. He spoke in English.

He was a contractor, he said, and was willing to undertake the work on my drive.

Gravel would be needed and a ton of metal; his own team was working nearby so it would not be much trouble getting them over. He named a price and I agreed to it without dispute. How long would it take? He said if his men started working first thing the next morning, the drive should be ready in three days. I agreed that he should commence the next day.

The house-painters completed their work on the afternoon of the second day. They wanted to go back to Nakuru, and if I saw them to the station and put them on the train, they could find their own way, they said. One of the *shamba* boys wished to return too, for there was no more work to be done. I engaged a taxi and took all three to Nairobi station, bought them their tickets and put them on the night train to Nakuru.

When I returned to Much Binding I found the estate agent waiting for me. He had a prospective tenant with him. The drive was now in such good condition that the tenant had actually driven his car down it and there it was parked tidily away on the side of the house behind a thicket of poinsettia.

I was glad to inform the agent and the tenant that the drive would be completed by the next day. The tenant asked permission to leave his car where it was. The agent, who had come along in his own car, would give him a lift back to his hotel. The next afternoon he would be back round about four to take possession of the house. His wife was visiting relatives in Limuru. He would come along with her in her car.

The lease and other matters were left to the agent to tie up. When they left I went next door, Napoleon keeping faithfully to my side, and, asking permission to use the telephone, I rang up Billy. I told him I was ready to come home again. His fears had been in vain, I said. All had gone well. It was a pity we could not sell Much Binding, but at least we had a tenant and the rent was good. I felt like celebrating, I said.

"You go straight back to the house," Billy said. "Lock yourself in and stay there till I come."

But he wouldn't be able to get to Nairobi till about three the next afternoon. I couldn't see myself twiddling my thumbs in a locked house, just waiting.

For the first time in weeks I slept long

and late into the morning. The contractor and his men arrived. I could hear them working on the drive outside. I knew that the lights on the front verandah and the back were still burning, but I didn't care. Those lights were left on as a precautionary measure. No terrorist, I argued, would care to be spotted should he wish to attack in the night. Neither would any dare to break one of the lamps, because the police patrol would notice its absence and come over to inquire. Napoleon slept in the room with me. I felt I could trust him to give timely warning.

All things considered, those nights at Much Binding had held little terror for me.

It was in the daytime, when all the *Bwanas* and the *Memsaabs* went off to work, when their houses were left empty and their large gardens as untenanted and silent as graveyards, that twinges of fear pinched along my nerves. Murder could be done between breakfast and lunch, or lunch and tea, and who would there be to hear a cry for help?

I think I can honestly say that I was the only European woman in that part of Spring Valley who remained behind during office hours. The knowledge was far from comforting.

When I went outside on to the enclosed verandah the drive was completed and the contractor stood at the door. It was about ten o'clock. Every European had left two hours earlier for the office. Spring Valley was locked in its mid-morning emptiness.

Seeing me appear at the steel-mesh partition of the verandah, the contractor came over. His men were squatting on the side of the drive, all watching me with eyes narrowed against the strong light. There was a sinister quality to that staring, to that silence which fell upon them at the sight of me. Eighteen men against one woman. Oh no, I thought. I am staying behind the steel-mesh.

"Well," said the contractor, very jocular, very bright this morning, "what do you think of your drive now?"

He had done well and deserved to be congratulated. I would pay him his money at once. I had it with me. He pretended not to see the bundle of notes I pushed through the steel-mesh.

"Come and walk on the drive," he said. "See how good we make it. Come outside."

I shook my head, conveying that I was too busy. I said I was leaving that afternoon and had all the packing to get through between now and then. I told him I had added a twenty-shilling tip for him because I was so pleased with his work.

One of his men asked him a question in Kikuyu. He answered him shortly. There was something pleasant and friendly about this contractor. If he was a Mau Mau, and perhaps one highly placed in the terrorist hierarchy, sworn to kill a dozen instead of one European, I felt that he didn't enjoy the rôle very much. When he took the money there was something like real gratitude in his eyes.

My packing did not take me long. I cooked myself a light meal and ate it. Napoleon had his raw beef and made yelping little cries to be let out of the house. When I opened the door he was away in a flash.

I went out into the garden. It was shortly after one o'clock, and down every drive in Spring Valley cars were speeding home, everyone hurrying to snatch a meal before getting back to the office by two o'clock. Traffic trams in Nairobi were getting worse every day.

It was a beautiful day. Any premonition of fear I might have had earlier on vanished in the bright, cold atmosphere. The air smelled of cypress and eucalyptus. Far, far away over the *vlei*, beyond the dark line of the forest, was Mount Kenya. By evening I should be able to catch a glimpse of her glittering white summit from Nakuru.

Soon the cars were wending their way back. Servants hurried through their work, slammed doors and went out on their afternoon stroll round town. Napoleon was nowhere within sight.

Presently I felt the little twinges pinching along my nerve-ends again. Not a soul was about. Gardens and houses were quite empty, deserted. I tried to listen in case I could catch the sound of voices, for in the cold rare air of the Highlands sound travels great distances. But not so much as a murmur broke the silence.

I had strolled far down the garden. The thought of running back to the house occurred to me, but I realised how silly I would look even in my own eyes. There was a quality to the silence, the stillness, that was beginning to unnerve me.

I saw coming across the *vlei* from two

directions, and converging upon me, two men who might have been houseboys, except that they both wore raincoats. It was a bright day, and what houseboy would wear a raincoat when he was doing the town, resplendent in his best clothes? I looked about me, beginning to make my way with decent slowness towards the house. But the house was a good three hundred yards or so away as yet.

A third man, also wearing a raincoat, was walking towards Much Binding, stepping casually over fences, trampling unconcernedly over flower-beds. All the men had their hands in their pockets. They quickened their pace when they saw me watching them.

I quickened my pace a little too. Terrorists were short of guns. If these men were terrorists the weapons concealed in their raincoats would be *pangas*. One cut grass with *pangas*, chopped firewood. Since the outbreak of terrorism they had become famous, for it was with the *panga* that human bodies were slashed and animals maimed.

I was within a hundred yards of the house when the Kikuyu contractor appeared round the corner, stepping quickly to cut off my retreat. He too wore a raincoat and his hands also were thrust deep into his pockets. I could not help glancing down at the raincoat. He moved quickly towards me and I distinctly saw the shape of a *panga* blade outlined under the raincoat.

"Hullo," I called. To my astounded ears my voice sounded quite normal, even as if I were pleased to see him. I smiled, lifting my hands as if to shade my eyes from the sun. He could see I had no gun, I thought, so it was not worth killing me if it was only fire-arms he wanted. My gun was safely tucked under my clothes in the cuitcase.

"What's brought you here?" I spoke softly, as if we might be overheard. I glanced significantly in the direction of the house. He slowed down and followed my glance.

It was my turn to step forward. I went straight towards him, finger on lips. The man's eyes were feverish. I had often seen that same feverish light in Gushu's eyes. But his were also dilated, lids opened wide, glance unfocused, unnaturally bright. A little saliva had gathered in the corner of his mouth and trickled down, but he did

313

nothing about it, just went on grinning and grinning. I kept my eyes fixed on his.

We stared at each other. He could do nothing but grin away, while the saliva trickled freshly down his chin. He looked hysterical, a little mad, I thought. He was fast losing control as I walked slowly towards him. I could see, without looking, that the other three men had paused.

"What do you want now?" I whispered, again glancing at the house. "A first-class reference? I will get the three *bwanas* in there" — again I nodded towards the house — "to sign one for you. They all admire your drive very much indeed."

The man halted in his tracks. Indecision was followed by the realisation that this thing he had to do, which was repugnant to him and which filled him with terror, need not be done. He blinked.

My own senses were very much on the alert, and my mind worked so quickly and yet so calmly that I had an impression of everything happening in slow motion. Without looking I saw that the other three had also stopped, watchful, cautious.

"Well? Is it a reference you want, then?" He had no control over his voice. When he answered his words squeezed out of a compressed voice-box, husky, inaudible. He swallowed and tried again. This time the tone was pitched high, the voice too loud.

"Work. Is more work here for me? I come see."

He had been told that there was no more work for him at Much Binding several times already. He knew very well that I was leaving that day and going back upcountry.

"Sh! Not so loud! Those three *bwanas* in there — see the car they came in? Tucked under the kitchen windows? They are fixing up the sale of this house."

The station wagon had lain parked under the kitchen windows behind the poinsettias since the previous evening. It would not be visible from the drive, where the contractor and his men had worked up till that morning. On the other hand, if he or his men had come round a little way for any reason at all, they would have spotted the vehicle at once.

On this one point — had that station wagon been observed or not? — hung my life.

To the unnatural acceleration of my

mental processes, time itself seemed to come to a stop. There were several impressions which impinged upon my consciousness as I stood confronting the Kikuyu, eyes not swerving from his. I was acutely aware of the cold, bright sunlight falling about me in crystal flakes; of the tips of the eucalyptus trees, where the branches tapered to a single stalk with young glossy red leaves, quivering in the light afternoon breeze: of the silence, the stillness.

"Three *bwanas* . . .? In the *nymbani*? There?" The contractor's mind, on the other hand, was working very slowly indeed, knotted up as it was in a complication of emotion, tension, terror and repugnance. I nodded. The vehicle had not been observed then. He was swallowing my lie.

Or was he? I still do not know the answer to that question.

But had I provided him with a good enough excuse for not going through with the killing? Suddenly I saw him sag before my eyes as if his bones had turned soft. With the back of his hand he wiped his mouth.

One of the three men barked out a question. He replied in the Kikuyu dialect — a couple of grunts and a cough. I was aware of movement again. The men began to walk away in different directions, moving rapidly.

"Come along now and let me get you that reference," I said, feeling that my own nerve was beginning to give way. Reaction would soon set in.

But the man shook his head. He made no pretence about the relief he felt. He turned and hurried away, leaving me there, alone at the bottom of the garden. Taking my time, I strolled back to the house. Only when I was inside, doors locked and bolted, did I begin to tremble. The trembling became a shudder. My first instinct was to pray. But even a prayer could not be formulated. I knelt by my bed, shaking all over.

Presently I felt a little more in control of myself. I went into the kitchen and drank some cold water out of the tap. While I was putting the cup away the new tenant arrived to take possession of the house. Five minutes later, having broken speed records on the Nairobi-Nakuru hundred-mile run, Billy swept down the drive, sounding a fanfare on his horn.

Once I was seated in the car beside him and the door shut, he turned a beaming, jubilant face on me. "Never, never, never again will I let you out of my sight! God, what I've been through! See these grey hairs? That's what you've done. Never again!"

10

OUR tour was nearly over. In a few weeks' time we would be making our last safaris, visiting loved places for the last time. There was now a sense of parting, of farewell, to the parties we gave, to the parties that were given for us. When our friends began to talk of "next year" or "when the next rains come" or "when we return from home leave", we kept silent. We no longer had a place in their plans, in Kenya's future.

"It will take us a long, long time," said Billy, "to get over Kenya. Our roots have gone too far down here. We are of an age when uprooting does not come easily."

It was indeed to take a long time, as we realise now. What a pity it is that hearts cannot obey the mind's cool judgement.

Mau Mau still raged, and killings still went on, but the back of the movement was broken. It was only a question of time before Kenya would be free of this unrest and people could walk again without fear.

In the small hours of the night, some time in late June, we were disturbed by the distant splutter of gunfire. We did not leave our beds to look across the lake towards the steep pastures beyond it. We knew what had caused the gunfire. The police and the Army had no doubt got on to the trail of a gang and were chasing it through the forests.

"The weekend Mau Mau at it again," Billy said sleepily. "Our spare-time terrorists giving the Forces a run for their money."

I dropped off to sleep wondering how these terrorists eluded screening.

Three busy days followed. Billy was due to go off to Maralal. The family were organised and conveyed to Kitale along with Anna. Packing was soon to begin in earnest and this meant that the time was at hand when we must choose what to take with us and what to sell or give away of all the impedimenta we had accumulated during our sojourn in Kenya.

Gushu was around, helping. He had little to say. When Billy showed him the bundle of clothing that was to be his on our departure, he showed neither pleasure nor satisfaction. This we dismissed as typical of the African temperament. During the past few days he had walked with a decided limp. But this again we ignored.

From my point of view the Maralal safari turned out to be a great success. Up in the high forests above the *boma* we filmed elephant at close range; out on the deserts to the north, the Grevy's zebra and the kudu, the gerenuk and the eland passed in obliging procession before the camera. We filmed a friendly set-to between two young elephants, with the rest of the herd munching and ear-flapping unconcernedly about them. On the way back up through the mountains to the *boma* of Maralal we made a film of a party of young Samburu *moran*, decked out in war-paint, carrying their slender spears and narrow shields, setting off on a lion hunt. The magnificent scenery, the birds, even the camp were all faithfully recorded in Kodachrome.

The first piece of news that greeted us on our return home was that Gushu was *mgonjwa*. With much satisfaction Kimanau, our Kipsigi boy, imparted this information. He had never got over the insult to his tribal status when he found himself — a member of an honoured pastoral tribe famous as warriors and hunters — engaged to work as No. 2 under Gushu, a Kikuyu.

Leaving Anna to get the children's supper, I followed Kimanau. It was quite early in the evening and the sun was still pouring its yellow flood of light from above the Mau range. The flamingoes were getting restive about the lake shores but as yet had made no move to rise and fly away to their nocturnal resting-place.

Kimanau beat on Gushu's door with vigour. "Open up! The *Memsaab* is here," he called in Swahili. We waited. Not a sound came from the room. Before he could bang again I stopped him. If anything was wrong, the Kipsigi's attitude would only make it worse.

I knocked and asked what was the matter. Gushu opened the door and then fell back on his bed in a sitting position. His legs were stretched straight out before him. Hastily he covered them with his blanket.

"Get out," he growled when Kimanau swaggered in. I suggested that our No. 2 had better go and lend a hand with unloading the safari tackle. Reluctantly Kimanau withdrew, but not beyond the bottom of the steps.

"What's wrong, Gushu? Are you ill?"

He shook his head, drooping over himself. His skin was paper-dry and a greyish colour. The eyeballs like red coals had fallen deep into the hollow sockets. For months now Gushu had been no more than skin and bone; now his features were more anthropoid than ever, resembling the ape rather than the giraffe.

"If you don't tell me, how can I help you?"

He muttered under his breath. Then repeated, "You cannot help me," in English.

"Why don't you let me try? You are ill. You need help. What has happened?"

He raised his head a little. The feverish eyes went to the door. I promptly shut it, nearly catching Kimanau's much-ringed ear-lobe. One of the *shamba* boys had settled himself for a grandstand view through the window. With the threat of instant dismissal if he returned, I packed him off to water the plants.

"Now then. No more nonsense. You are

323

ill, Gushu, and I must know what it is. Or do you want to be sent off to hospital?"

His mind seemed to be wandering a little. He begged not to be sent to hospital. Not to hospital, not to hospital. . . .

"We won't send you to hospital, then," I promised. "But you must let us help you. You are in pain. We cannot let you sit here and suffer. Gushu, trust us. We are your friends. Your old friends, Gushu. Trust us."

"You are my friend," he said, his mind wandering a little. Then he raised those terrible eyes and looked at me. "There is a fight. Bad mens wants me to do bad things. I say 'no'. Then I run away. They throw spears and one catch my leg. I pull it out and run away."

Africans constantly fought among themselves. One did not interfere or ask questions. "Never mind about that now. Show me the wound."

His head hung. Almost as if it acted on its own volition, one black claw of a hand drew aside the blanket revealing a gangrenous wound about four inches above the left ankle. The smell of putrefaction nearly sent me flying out of the room.

"It is finish. You cannot help me, *Memsaab*. Finish."

"We won't let you die," I said. "It isn't finished."

I kept repeating over and over again that he was going to get well. It was absolutely essential for him to believe in his own recovery. If an African feels that a doom is upon him, either by magic or by any other power, he will sit himself down and quietly die away. Gushu nodded. "Ah so," he said. "You will make me well. My *Bwana* and *Memsaab* make me well."

When I opened the door Kimanau nearly tumbled into the room. On the way back to the house he walked companionably by my side. "What is the matter with that Kikuyu? Bad lot, the Kikuyu."

"He's caught a fever," I said.

Billy had already bathed and changed and was pouring out our sundowners when I went into the drawing-room. He listened to what I had to say. "Poor brute," he said. "Poor, poor brute."

We had a well-stocked medicine chest. Billy took all he might need, from penicillin tablets to bandages, antiseptics, and so on, and while I kept Kimanau spraying imaginary mosquitoes in the guest house, he slipped off to Gushu's room. Ten o'clock that night he went again. And again early in the morning. During the day, when Billy was away at the office, I took over.

Slowly, very slowly, Gushu began to recover. Every time Kimanau's sardonic eye fell on the bowls of soup, the plates of food that were taken to Gushu, he made cutting remarks in his Kipsigi dialect to one of the *shamba* boys, not caring whether the other, a fellow from the shores of Lake Victoria, understood him or not.

Ten days later Gushu was able to limp outside again, but he kept to the servants' part of the *shamba*. One Tuesday afternoon, when I was supposed to be having my siesta, I went into the servery to see if there was sufficient pumpkin pie in the refrigerator to serve at dinner. I usually made two or three at a go and dished them up at judiciously spaced intervals.

Gushu was standing by the ki-apple hedge, obviously waiting for someone. The rest of our servants had gone off to the Bondeni and would not return until tea-time. Keeping out of view, I waited to see what was going to happen.

A man was coming down the footpath which skirted the hedge. When he drew near he slackened his pace, but appeared not to notice Gushu, who, very much on the alert, had moved up against the hedge. At once I recognised the fellow on the other side of the hedge.

The vertical, midday equatorial sunlight cut his features into sharp lanes, highlighting the cheekbones, the nose flat at the ridge, flaring like an animal's round the nostrils, the rims of the thick, out-thrust bottom lip, the narrow ape-brow. This was the fellow I had seen that night when the noises in the roof drove me out of the house and I had come upon a gathering in Gushu's rooms. This was the one who had harangued the rest, his hands resting on a Kikuyu *simi*.

Now, as he drew level with Gushu, he said something. I did not see Gushu make reply. The man paused then and, turning his head a fraction, spoke again. This time Gushu merely turned his back and limped away.

For a moment it seemed as if the other would follow. He made a quick, furious movement in the direction of the little gate, but seemed to change his mind. In a few seconds he was on his way again, going down towards the town.

In those days Billy and I often played a few rounds of golf together. Friends used to tease us about this. But the fact was that we found these games relaxing. Billy could have as many trial shots as he liked, while I enjoyed the wonderful scenery. We enjoy each other's company and Billy thinks my jokes funny.

That evening we had a round together. The Nakuru golf course is laid out on the middle slopes of Menengai on the north flank. It undulates in great zig-zags, overlooking distractingly magnificent scenery. It was more tempting to rest the eyes on the violet march of the great western escarpment, the lapis lazuli lake, the shifting clouds of flamingoes, the silent hills, than on a small perverse white ball that never went where it should. Just before sunset there always came a moment when the forces of earth and sky gathered into a transcendent glory, when the human heart expanded till it seemed to encompass all creation. A moment out of eternity, breathless with prayer.

The seventeenth faced westwards, faced into the full tide of the sun's last beams. We had teed off and were walking side by side, when all of a sudden a terrible coldness came over me. My brain was drenched in a misery such as I had never known.

"Billy," I whispered. "Wait." It is impossible to describe the sense of utter desolation that overcame my whole being.

"What is it?"

I was blinded and deafened by this strange thing that was happening. I came out of a sort of trance to hear him ask again: "What is it? You're as white as a sheet."

The words of explanation wouldn't come. "What is the matter? Are you ill?" he kept repeating.

Within minutes I was myself again, a little shaken and more than a little bewildered.

"Gushu is dead," I announced.

"What?" He thought I was crazy. How could I know such a thing?

"I know Gushu is dead." Just as I had known on other occasions in my life of things that had happened to friends of mine even when they were far from me; as

I had known not long ago, the moment Mary Pope's operation was over, that she was going to get well again; so now I knew beyond any shadow of a doubt that poor Gushu was dead.

We did not finish that round. We took a short cut back to the club-house, had a double whisky each, and went straight home. The first thing Billy did was to ask the other servants to fetch Gushu. They came back to say he was not in his room, not anywhere to be seen.

"This is sheer lunacy, of course," Billy said, and got back into the car and went off to make inquiries at the police station. No one answering Gushu's description had been taken in, certainly no one like that found dead. He even made inquiries at the Native Civil Hospital, persuading the Indian doctor, who happened to be there on his rounds, to let him see the two new cases that had come in that day. No Gushu.

Kimanau served dinner, looking like a cat with a canary in its mouth.

That night I slept as if I had been drugged. It was a wonderful sleep, deep, fathoms deep. When I awoke at six as usual the next morning I felt years younger. At this distance of time, it seems to me like recovering from a grave illness.

On the afternoon of that same day, Billy was called upon to identify the body of an African. It turned out that the man had locked himself inside the house of a friend, while the friend was away, and had hanged himself from the roof beam. What furniture the friend possessed had been stacked up against the door after it had been locked from the inside. The window was barred. No one could get in or out that way.

Gushu had died by his own hand. As far as the police surgeon could fix the time of death, it had occurred the previous evening.

On the 31st of July, 1954, we boarded a plane at the Nairobi airport. We arrived in London the next day. On August 28th we sailed for Canada in the *Empress of France*.

Kenya may be several thousand miles away. But what is distance to those who cherish their memories? For us who cannot forget all that happened, it seems as if we have been away no more than a matter of hours. . . .

THE END